IRELAND

towards a sense of place

University College, Cork

IRELAND

towards a sense of place

The UCC-RTE Lectures

edited by

Joseph Lee

Cork University Press
1985

First published in 1985 by
Cork University Press, University College, Cork

ISBN 0 902561 35 9

Frontispiece courtesy Gladys Leach
Cover design by Maria Kennedy

Printed in the Republic of Ireland by Tower Books,
86 South Main St., Cork

Contents

Joseph Lee

Preface

This book originated as a series of lectures sponsored by Radio Telefís Éireann and University College, Cork, and delivered in UCC in January 1985. It follows a series of televised lectures in the Faculty of Arts in UCD in 1984, boldly begun on the initiative of Professor Breandán Ó Buachalla, and subsequently published as an issue of the *Crane Bag* under the title *Ireland: Dependence and Independence.*

University scholars in the humanities and social sciences have not always been sufficiently conscious of their responsibility to transmit their findings to the wider public. Nor has RTE always been sufficiently conscious of a responsibility to stimulate informed public discussion by means other than the mere adversarial posturing of the spokemen for vested interests. There are, it has to be conceded, major difficulties for both scholars and broadcasters in this area. The scholar fears the sacrifice of standards, while the broadcaster must fear the sacrifice of audiences. However, it can be argued that neither problem is insuperable, and certainly neither will be surmounted until they are confronted. Both the scholars and the broadcasters can continue to learn from the experiment that began in UCD, continues in modified form in this series, and in which other institutions of higher learning will, I hope, participate in future.

RTE is sometimes reproached for remaining too Dublin orientated. The *Irish Times* neatly, if unconsciously, reflects this Dublin fixation when, in correctly stressing the importance of the role of the Director General of RTE in moulding national thinking, it commented that 'The impact on the public consciousness of the workings of the mind of the Director General is more easily measured than that of the President of University College, Dublin, and the Provost of Trinity College, Dublin put together'.[1] Thus are the presidents of

---

[1] *Irish Times,* 4 March 1985.

UCC, UCG and Maynooth patronisingly consigned to oblivion by media decree! This venture, therefore, marks a welcome attempt to survey aspects of Irish experience, past and present, from a perspective rarely enough reflected in the opinion programmes of RTE.

It may help readers evaluate the contents if they know something of the background of the contributors, for these essays are intensely personal statements. Biographical details are contained in the 'Notes on contributors' at the end of the book. Suffice it to say that although five were born in Munster (only Dr. Dooley from America being denied that privilege!), if any group should be indifferent to the demands of place, it is this one, for the world of international scholarship is their intellectual, and frequently their physical, home. They have lodged at length not only on the Lee, but on Cam and Thames, Rhine and Seine, Charles and Chicago, Ohio and St. Lawrence, even on Nile and Euphrates. They have all drunk deep of the springs of other cultures. None need have chosen to return, or to come, to Ireland. While in this year of 'Cork 800' it is not inappropriate that UCC scholars should experience a heightened awareness of place, nevertheless their commitment is cerebral as well as emotional.

The theme of this volume is the sense of place, vague or precise, mundane or romantic, real or imaginary, in the Irish mind, with reference both to place within Ireland, and to Ireland's place in the world. The contributors, concerned with psychic no less than physical space, seek to excavate the sense of place, as they probe various layers of perception — geographical, literary, ethical, legal, economic and political. John Kenneth Galbraith is reported to have said recently (after these lectures were delivered) that 'The greatest problem of Ireland is where people decided to locate it'.[2] Many of our contributors had already analysed one implication of that fate. The problem of Irish exposure to English influence is a recurring theme throughout the series.

Observers of the Irish people's sense of their own place in the world are bound to wonder at times about the clarity of Irish perceptions. Readers may find some of the verbal sorties scattered through the book provocatively vigorous, but the tone of criticism that occasionally surfaces is not one of dismissive contempt, but rather one

---

[2] *Irish Times*, 2 March 1985.

of exasperated commitment. That is hardly avoidable, given that we want to ask not only what has been achieved, but what could have been and what ought to have been achieved in our circumstances.

Affection for our country is accompanied by pride in our own subjects. This is eloquently conveyed in the proud defiance of Professor Smyth's description of his discipline, geography, as a 'naive' subject — 'naive' because it strives for the impossible, and continues to reach for the stars. Every sentence of Professor Smyth's invocation of a sense of place can be read as a manifesto proclaiming his passionate belief in the contribution of geography to the creation of the civilised conscience.

While we would all confess to being passionately in love with our subjects, I would like to think that none of us is the prisoner of our passion. That would be unworthy of humanists, who must always seek to preserve a sense of proportion, and to transcend 'the parochialism of the present', whether in time or place, and to help expand the frontiers of the future by transmitting the essence of the past. We therefore strive to use our subjects as a means towards a deeper understanding of the nature of Irish society, and of our national personality. Sceptics may query the resilience of that personality, as it is increasingly exposed to destructive utilitarian influences. We take issue with the utilitarians, with the parrot-like cry for 'relevance' in education, not on the grounds that 'relevance' is beneath the university man, but rather on the grounds that, as Professor Patrick Lynch, following Maritain, has reminded us, 'the problem with the utilitarian view is that it is not utilitarian enough'.[3] Those who most stridently invoke 'relevance' have, characteristically, shirked research into the 'relevance' of the demand for 'relevance'. In this context, it is worth noting Professor Wrigley's demonstration that management stands in the mainstream of humane studies, that it renders its most effective contribution to the quality of economic performance when it triumphs over the temptation to service short term 'needs', insists on its identity as an intellectual discipline, and places man rather than the machine at the centre of its concern.

This insistence on the importance of intellect is a third theme that emerges from these contributions. Ireland has suffered not so much

---

[3] P.K. Lynch, 'Whither Science Policy', *Administration*, 27, 3 (Autumn 1979) p. 257.

from an anti-intellectual culture as from a non-intellectual one. Apart from the consequent cultural impoverishment, it may have paid a heavy price in purely material terms. It has lacked the intelligence to mobilise the natural talent of its people, and therefore now languishes as an unsuccessful socio-economic entity, trundling along with only half the per capita income of northern Europe. In this respect the current fetish with the 'high tech' sector, however desirable and impressive technological development may be, and however radical its prophets feel themselves to be, is in the central tradition of national mindlessness. It is high time to foster a tradition of intellectual enquiry, which this country generally so conspicuously lacks, in the cause not only of national dignity but of national efficiency.

The rediscovery of a sense of place seems likely to be a central tendency in European thought in the late twentieth century. The environmental movement is but one symptom of this. As European man gropes for psychological security in a restless world, grasping at last that unlimited material progress, desirable though it be in its own right, cannot provide fulfilment in his search for personal identity, a feeling for place, so often dismissed as a mere symptom of parochialism, now comes to be seen as an integral part of the consciousness of civilised man. In this connection it is instructive to note the recent re-evaluation of the Impressionist sense of place, superbly captured in the exhibition in the Grand Palais in Paris that opened a week after the delivery of these lectures.[4]

In the course of their meditations on a sense of place, the authors reassert the importance of the aeonian challenge that confronts man about the nature of his own being. Issues of identity, individual and collective — who am I?, who are we? — issues of morality, of man's relationship with his fellows and with his God, the abiding questions of the human condition, lie at the centre of our concern.

The papers were composed independently. No attempt has been made to impose any uniformity of view or of style. Indeed, the attentive reader will detect not only differences of emphasis, but directly contradictory views, between various authors. The lectures have been slightly revised for publication, and where the time constraint of television obliged speakers to omit material relevant to their

---

[4] *L'impressionnisme et le paysage français*, Paris, 1985.

argument, they have incorporated this into their notes.

One of the compensations of a collective enterprise of this type is that it enables the editor to accumulate a wide range of debts. Our producer, Mick McCarthy, and assistant producer, Marie Travers, succeeded in delicately combining exhortation with forbearance. In moments of despondency, the laggards amongst us drew sustenance from their quiet confidence that we would meet our deadlines! We are also grateful for the support of Muiris MacConghail and Seán Ó Mórdha in RTE, who refused to settle for the safe option. The President of UCC, Professor Tadhg Ó Ciardha, enthusiastically endorsed the idea of close cooperation with RTE. The Vice-President's Secretary, Eileen Fehily, has placed me even further in her debt by responding with characteristic efficiency and good humour to yet another barrage of importunate demands. Professor Seán Lucy, who has himself so illuminatingly explored the literature of place, brought an elegant sense of style to the chairing of the lectures. Christy Moriarty, Assistant-Superintendent of General Services, attended efficiently to the lecture arrangements. The Secretary of Cork University Press, Donal Counihan, dealt imperturbably with the variety of unforeseen circumstances seemingly inseparable from collective endeavour!

Seán Daly has not only been printer, but virtual joint-editor, as he has coped with the editor's own peculiar sense of place during the preparation of the volume for publication.

I am very grateful to them all.

1 *William J. Smyth*

Explorations of Place

On the back cover of the standard school exercise-book of the nineteen-fifties, *An Cóipleabhar Caighdeánach*, a map of the island of Ireland — Éire — was depicted. It clearly marked out the old provincial boundaries of Cúige Uladh, Cúige Connachta, Cúige Laighean agus Cúige Mumhan. Those of us over forty were introduced to *Tír Eolaíocht* through this map. How one loved to trace freehand the complicated, intimate outline of the Irish coast, trying to remember the different shapes of Uibh Rathach and Corca Dhuibhne, then on past Loop Head, to contrast the sharp granitic edge of Cois Fharraige with the complex mosaic of islands and peninsulas that stretched from Conamara through Clew Bay and on to the Mullet; then curving north around the Rosses and the Fanad peninsula, past the bony dog's head of Inis Eoghain and the estuaries of the Swilly and the Foyle. Swinging southwards, we probed the Ards Peninsula with its memories of Viking raids, and the Cooley Peninsula with its echoes of the ancient Irish epic of the *Táin Bó Cuailgne*; on past the smooth east coast, where the mouths of the Boyne and the Liffey provided tempting access to the invader, from Newgrange builders to Dublin office-block developers. Then, rounding Carnsore point, our pencils explored the deep harbours of Waterford and Cork, and that highly-indented South-West coast until Valentia and the Blaskets swam into view again.

It was an early introduction to the complexity of the shapes of places along Ireland's coast. Missing from the map were the inland seas — Seamus Heaney's soft secretive boglands — which defined other islands and peninsulas throughout the inner heart of the island.[1] The bogs also defined townlands, parishes, tuatha, baronies, counties, even provinces. The school-map also excluded the complex massifs and mountains which further divided Ireland into a whole

1

series of uplands and lowlands, which in turn nurtured a wide range of distinctive communities and ways of living across the island. Missing from the map were the rivers which (with the fossilised river systems — the eskers) provided the oldest arteries of communication, and still focus different parts of Ireland around particular river and port towns. Missing too were the roads, canals and railways, which often cut across these river basins to link up the major cities and in particular to pull so much towards Dublin and, to a lesser extent, Belfast. This school map — while showing the thirty-two counties — did not show the political frontier, the Border, almost as though the mapmaker did not recognise its existence or hoped that it would soon vanish.

Maps often reveal more about their makers by what they leave out than by what they include. Our school map placed Éire/Ireland in splendid isolation. It did not show the proximity of the North-Eastern part of the island to Scotland, nor the proximity of Eastern Ireland, to Chester and onwards to London. The possibilities of interconnections between South-Eastern Ireland and South Wales and the West Country were not suggested. Likewise, the map, reflecting our cultural lenses, did not open out to encompass the orientation of the South coast to the European mainland curving westwards from Nantes, Bordeaux, Spain, the Mediterranean and on to the other end of the old Indo-European world.[2] Far out across the Atlantic was that New World of America, which the people from the west reduced down to size by calling it the next parish. Boston, New York, and Philadelphia were physically distant from these communities, but culturally very close, linked by the powerful bonds of kinship, monies, and the letters which exchanged across the ocean the stories of life and death in the old townland and the New World city ghetto.

Our schoolbooks did, however, carry symbols of Celtic Ireland — the Round Tower, the Harp, the Hound; and therefore carried a selective view of ourselves as a people. Today I notice that the schoolbook cover may often carry a map of the European Economic Community, with *all* the countries' names written in *English*. This map places Ireland in a much wider perspective; and there are more copybooks now, accountbooks, graph books, science books. The student is being asked to see himself or herself as belonging to a wider, more specialised, more ordered, more efficient world. And yet when I look at our daughter's primary school history book, I note in the context of Irish stories that, after the five tales of the Fiannaíocht, the selection leaps from the capture of St. Patrick to Aodh Ruadh O'Donnell's escape, to Daniel O'Connell in court. There is nothing about the contribution of the Vikings, nothing about the Norman feudal inheritance; silence about the seventeenth-century upheavals and settlements.[3] There seems to be conflicting messages here. We are expected to be modern — to engage the world — without knowing fully who we are, where we have come from, or where we now stand as a society in the world. Have we lost our sense of place? — for a sense of place is bound up with memory, identity, caring; with articulating the true nature of our past experiences so as to enable us, more creatively, to engage the present, and through that the future.

There is also another mapping tradition. High up on one of the stained-glass windows of this university theatre, the figures of Ptolemy, Columbus and, probably, Mercator are depicted. It was Mercator who projected this round earth onto a flat map, re-drawing the lines of latitude and longitude so as to enable sailors and navigators, colonists and empire-builders to steer confidently through the great seas, and conquer new lands.[4] Ireland's long-standing status as a colony has therefore meant that the cold, clinical eye of the colonial cartographer has long gazed upon and defined the island. For example, the great Civil and Down surveys of the mid-seventeenth century — basically a collection of Cromwellian ledger-books and maps — list the names of the former occupiers, classify them according to their religious *cum* ethnic status, and detail the size and quality of their properties, before transferring these properties to the new conquering elites. These maps and documents are triumphant symbols of the power of the colonial government to penetrate and appropriate every corner, every placename and every person in the land. These materials also show the newly centralising English state bureaucracy shaping the worlds it encountered to better fit its image of what a 'proper' language, economy and society should sound, work and behave like.[5]

Today, we can use these documents for two different purposes: through them we can reconstruct the varied impact of the Cromwellian settlement; equally they allow us to penetrate beneath the flat map and the flattening categories, to reconstruct the rich and varied worlds that were lost, or often, only partially lost, in the seventeenth century. For example, the new landlord culture was to sweep many old villages from the land and create a new imperial Augustan landscape centered on the Big House and the plantation/landlord town. Yet, as in County Tipperary, which at best was only half-conquered, many older settlements and social structures survived this period, providing the backbone of later resurgence.[6]

The map remains however, both flat and static. It does not capture the rounded sense of place as experienced by the insider. This experience involves all the senses — of seeing, feeling, of sound, of touch and taste. The map does not capture the Proustian smell of the hayfields and the cowhouse, the ritual of the calendar feasts, of places saturated with pain and love, meanness and meaning, Neither does the map capture the excitement and roguery of the market, the squalor and the songs of the back streets, the variety of human life in city, town and kitchen.

Geography is a naive kind of discipline, even a foolish one, since it tries to marry these two perspectives: the outsider-perspective of the map, and the subjective, felt world of place. There is therefore always a tension in the discipline, and particularly in cultural geography, between knowing the world and experiencing it, between scholarly distance and caring, between truth and love.[7] My business for the remainder of this paper is to excavate a little into the archaeology of the Irish consciousness of places, to communicate the totality and complexity of a few of these places, and based on these experiences, to suggest a few pathways of creativity which we can, perhaps, forge towards the future.

From the beginning, I think, it is necessary to recognise that much of our lives — our experience of place — is a local thing. International, national and regional forces, for example, whether of today or yesterday, are mediated through the day-to-day interactions of people 'on the ground'.[8] This is true, whether one talks of a rural parish, a country town, a port city, or even capital cities. Each of these places has its own layered geography which incarnates — makes physical — the experiences and aspirations of its people.

Our first visit is to the parish of Clogheen-Burncourt, located in the valley between the Galtees and the Knockmealdowns in South-West Tipperary. It is a parish which straddles the borders of a number of dioceses, counties and competing urban hinterlands. The old name of the parish is *Sean Rathan*; and unlike many Catholic parishes the medieval and the modern parish territories are almost coterminous. Shanrahan was Christianised from the great monastic city of Lismore. Shanrahan's patron saint is Saint Cathaldus or Cathal. Our first lesson in Irish place experience comes here. Saint Cathaldus went on pilgrimage to the Holy Land, and on his return stayed on at Taranto in Southern Italy. There, he is also the patron saint: still a vital figure, celebrated in festivals every year. In Shanrahan he is only a name for curious antiquarians, and the modern Catholic chapel, displaced by the Reformation to the adjacent landlord town of Clogheen, is dedicated not to St. Cathaldus but to St. Mary. Within Clogheen, the chapel built in 1740 yielded in 1830 to the 'Big Chapel' which was relocated on the Main Street, between the Military Barracks and the Courthouse, and well away from its old Chapel Lane site and its butchers' shops. These shifts in location and dedication tells us much about the new, rootless middle-class ethos of a reconstructed Irish Catholicism. One of our younger geographers, Kevin Whelan, has recently shown how the Catholic Church, after the dislocations of the Reformation and Plantations, had literally to reconstruct itself in the eighteenth and nineteenth centuries: many of its buildings, including perhaps four hundred chapel-villages, are on virgin sites, away from the old sacred centres.[9] Continental devotional cults (like the Little Flower or the Sacred Heart) displaced native cults (like that of St. Cathaldus) which went back to the early Christian era. The new Church became part of the more commercialised, urban-based, thrifty, utilitarian, almost Nonconformist English-speaking Ireland, emerging triumphant between an ebbing Gaelic world on the one hand and an unsympathetic colonial one on the other. Imperial yes, the Catholic Church was also part of the decolonisation process, then helping to restore confidence and dignity to a people.[10]

Any place embodies many historical periods in its buildings, institutions and stories. The old parish centre of Shanrahan today is not the vital core of the Catholic community there; but it is still a sacred place, since it is the burial-place for the generations of peoples who have lived in this part of Ireland. It represents a focal point in the landscape, linking this earthly place with heaven and the underworld in a way which preserves a medieval way of looking at life and death. Its viewpoint is not of Mercator's linear, secular progression, but rather points to the existence of other worlds where ancestors dwell. In rural Ireland, therefore, the funeral remains one of the greatest expressions of social life. Funerals are for the living as well as the dead, and the meeting-places of home, church, public-house and cemetery, associated with the rituals of the dead, bond together communities at specific times. Funerals also reveal all the nuances of kinship-networks, class and status, that Irish society is always so acutely attuned to. Shanrahan is therefore no mere ruin; it is a place invested with the symbols of the identity of many competing families and one enduring community.[11]

The graveyard, like the world outside, has also its hierarchies: from the high Celtic tombstones of the wealthy to the timbered anonymity of the poor. There are two central monuments in this graveyard. One is dedicated to Father Nicholas Sheehy; the other, now delapidated and vandalised, is the vault of the landlord family of the O'Callaghans. Fr. Sheehy was hanged in Clonmel, as a consequence of a clash over a whole range of issues — agrarian, sectarian and political — which were beginning to erupt in Ireland in the second half of the eighteenth century. Then the Catholic middle class began to challenge for more powerful positions, while at the same time the small cooperative farmers along the mountain townlands were becoming day-labourers, squeezed out as large grazier-farms were created in these areas of former common land. There is a monument to Nicholas Sheehy inside the Catholic church grounds in Clogheen town. Significantly, it was erected by Nationalists in 1870. In a way it is an ironic piece of landscape iconography, for in the 1760s the elite of the Catholic Church in Waterford and Lismore had little good to say of Fr. Sheehy or the Whiteboy movement. Sympathetic to the person of Nicholas Sheehy in 1766, opposed to the erection of the monument in 1870, the landlord's position in all of this is even more complicated. But that is another story.

We rewrite history selectively, and embed the myth in the landscape. But there is a crucial distinction between the broader culture of a people — its full sense of place — and this notion of ethnicity. The culture of a people is its *total* way of life; an ethnic definition abstracts a *few* key symbols of identity and perpetuates them as the markers of the group, despite a whole series of transformations in the peoples' ways of living. We are back again to the clash between how we see ourselves on ours schoolbook covers, and the more complex reality of everyday life.[12]

Thus, Father Sheehy remains a bonding symbol, a heroic figure celebrated in song, story and drama. Yet the symbol obscures the bitter struggles between big farmers, small farmers, and cottier-labourers for access to the god, land. Nevertheless, it was and is the strength of the extended farmer kin-group which gives such a rural society its resilient cellular character, and makes for a society of remarkable staying power. Thus, the autonomy of rural societies should not be under-estimated; and in conjunction with parishes and chapel communities, these elaborate and now geographically extensive kinship and neighbourhood networks can be mobilised in defence of a whole range of values.[13]

Now let us look at a larger place. The country town also had a powerful bonding role in Ireland. We will stay in Co. Tipperary to explore these worlds. As you know, Tipperary is an odd county, a great mosaic of lands, places and peoples.[14] The county straddles a whole series of border-lands; criss-crossed by major routeways, it ranges from the richest land in Europe (in the lower Suir valley) to poorer upland-regions and stretches from the central pastoral midlands almost to Waterford port. It is divided between three dioceses, two county administrative areas, and two planning regions. It is almost Celtic in the scattering of its centres of power yet each of the major colonial groups that have shaped the Irish mosaic have kept their vitality here.[15] Since it is 'the blue & gold' which gives symbolic unity to this diverse county, it is proper that centrally-located Thurles — the home of the GAA — should tell a little of its story.

Thurles, *Durlas Éile*: its name speaks of a Celtic fortress in the territory of *Éile Uí Fhógartaigh*. It is situated in the heart of the rich limestone plains of Mid-Tipperary, one of the strong river-towns of the Suir. The Norman Butlers planted a major garrison-town here, and studded the surrounding region with manors and castles. Yet the later tower-houses in this wider region may indicate the fusion of Gaelic and Norman cultural worlds in this tough frontier territory. Since Butler patronage — the Butler shield — survived in Thurles until well into the nineteenth century, it did not remain an alien town, set apart from the countryside like many plantation and landlord towns elsewhere. As in the seventeenth century, the family names of the present-day occupiers point to the long-standing interconnections between town and countryside. It is a town warmed and bounded by many kinship links; and its working-class areas contain long-tailed families who still support the individual in times of stress. The core of the town, as at present laid out, differs little from the enclosed walled town of the later middle ages. The town then had a threefold structure. First, a rich, merchantile core in what is now the equally rich and carefully renamed Liberty Square. Second, an artisan and milling quarter across the Suir bridge to the east where the site of the old Carmelite friary is now occupied by the Cathedral. Third, poorer suburbs outside the gates to the west which today includes the offices of the local newspaper, the 'Tipperary Star', Semple Stadium, the Greyhound track, the County Home, the railway station and further down the line, the Sugar Factory. Thurles, therefore, is a thriving industrial, commercial and service town, with its everyday life of office and factory, mart and market swirling around the monuments and icons of the previous century.[16]

Thurles is of course the colourful Mecca for Munster hurling Finals: a place therefore where illusions have often been shattered, and never more effectively than in the epic final between Cork and Tipperary in 1984. As a Tipperary man, I had to endure the jibes of our son, a Corkman, after that traumatic last five minutes. Father and son diverged. The son established his separate identity. It was a good moment.

The Gaelic Athletic Association may also have its own illusions. Like the Catholic Church, it transcends the political frontier; it combines, in an extraordinarily powerful way, the Catholic parish-framework, the county administrative system, and an attempt to express itself in Irish as well as in English. Like the Catholic Church, the GAA is therefore an extraordinary hybrid; but unlike the Church, it was (and perhaps still is) a seedbed of democratic procedures. However, there is much tension between the poetry, freedom and evolving skills of the games on the ground, and the official view of what these games symbolise in Irish society. This official symbolic role seems at times too heavy and static a weight for the games to bear. The values of the GAA grew out of a self-reliant, enterprising, tenant-farmer tradition in the exciting years of the 1880s. It still remains to be determined whether the GAA can adapt its vision so as to assimilate both the new stratas and varied leisure-worlds now opening up in the towns, and the new search for emancipation on the part of Irish women. The Catholic Church, whose nineteenth-century buildings so dominate Thurles, may share similar problems of adaptation and growth.

One of the creative aspects of Irish life is the dialectic between such inland capitals as Thurles and the port cities. The tension between Cork and Tipperary is therefore very old, and not confined to the hurling field. In part, it is a dialectic between culture of the city and the more introverted one of the countryside. Cork city is an extraordinary place, for it is a port city that is situated deep inland. It is located also in a borderland between red sandstone ridges and white limestone valleys; between a pastoral north and west and a tillage world to the east and south. Culturally, it is divided (as is Dublin) between a north side and a south side; it is, at once, enclosed and open, a centre and a periphery.

Today we can see Cork from at least three perspectives: there is the image of the IDA developer, attempting to sell this metropolitan region as the growth-centre for electronics and computers, a place, as one piece of publicity put it, where 'high technology is a way of life'.[17] In contrast, each Corkonian will have his or her own image of their beloved city, full of colourful nooks and crannies, including, for them, home, street, school, pub, church or chapel; and such visible landmarks as Shandon, the 'Pana' (Patrick Street), the Coal Quay, St. Finbarr's, the Mardyke, FitzGerald's Park or the Lough — each person with their own special ensemble of places and peoples but all of them integrated around the banks of the Lee.[18]

But like all rivers, the braided Lee divides as well as it unites. It is perceived as a real territorial divide between the hurling worlds of the Glen (Rovers) to the north and (St. Finn) Barrs to the south. More critically, the river is seen as a symbolic divide between the intimate working-class street cultures of the 'north-side' (this culture zone of Corporation housing estates, criss-crossed by strong kinship and marriage links, actually extends southwards across the river to include Ballyphehane, Togher and Pouladuff) and the more detached, private, middle-class cultures of the 'south-side' (which also have both old and new cultural outliers north of the river). By virtue of its rosary of encircling hills, every Corkonian has many vantage points to read off his or her own acutely sensitive mental map of the status and category of each community in the city which is now five times as extensive as it was in 1900. Blackrock, Douglas and Bishopstown — each with an old village core — are now seen to be dominated by middle-class suburban townscapes in contrast to both the more variegated and complex inner city communities of South Parish, the

Lough, Shandon, Blarney Street and Blackpool and in more sharp contrast with the first, second and third generation of Corporation estates and family structures that stretch from 'Red City'/Garrán na mBrathar, Farran Rí and Mayfield on to Knocknaheeny and Hollyhill. Each Corkonian will read into these names a whole series of meanings as to housing types, schooling patterns, work or no work routines — indeed lifestyles as a whole. There are many dimensions to this cultural map but a basic polarity exists between the bowling, beagling and drag-hunting cultures of the old north side and the sailing, golfing, tennis and bridge-playing world of the southern suburbs, between a more oral-centered culture which prefers to scan the *Evening Echo* to one that favours the *Cork Examiner* and the *Irish Times*, from a culture that utilises public transport for day trips to Youghal or the 'Crosser' (Crosshaven) to those who travel abroad on holidays; in short between a world of 'localites' and a world of aspiring 'cosmopolites'.[19]

Mediating between the abstract Mercator view of the developer, and the subjective world of the native resident, the cultural geographer — even if he is a 'foreigner' — might emphasise the things that epitomise both the wholeness and the fragmentation of city life. *Corcach Laoi* — the marsh of the Lee — tells us that (if I might be permitted a soft, bilingual Joycean pun) Cork's '*bog*inning was in the void' of outwash channels and alluvium, which left an island site as a crucial crossing point between the ridges to the north and south. When you come to Cork, you will notice that it never stops raining, but you will also notice the extraordinary mildness of its winters, which allows grass to grow for eleven months in the year, in sharp contrast to the frost-bitten midlands, not to speak of the colder, bleaker North. Lying deep inland, Cork commands the rich sheltered ridge and valley grasslands of South Munster. These provide an ideal environment for the dairying herds. It was the butter, beef and pork trade that literally made this Atlantic city in the eighteenth century. This trade reclaimed the marshes, saw the city and port expand eastwards with its new rational gridiron streets still locked within the older curved channels and gentle island boundaries.[20]

This eastward move left intact the city's memory: that is, the old medieval core with its triangular structure: the fortressed Shandon, *Sean-dún*, the Irishtown through which the great drover-roads (the *bó-thair*) from the North converged on the city; second, the walled, oval-shaped island core, the 'flat' of the city, cross-girdled by its merchants' main street and many lanes; and, third, located on the southern ridge, the ancient monastic core of St. Finbarr's/Gillabbey, from which the Church ruled. One can still peel back all the layers of Cork's history and identity in the present urban fabric.

The pastoral heritage still lingers on in the city. Cork's musical heritage is not only a product of the operatic singers who visited the opera-house from the transatlantic liners (and incidentally made opera a city-wide rather than a middle-class thing in Cork). The enthusiasm in Cork for music is also a product of a leisurely pastoral society, which like all such cultures (Arabic, Indic, Hungarian) favoured music, song, poetry, drama, (the short story?) and the dance. One notes, too, that the city is full of dogs: in fact, Cork has probably the highest density of dogs per population of any European city. To sum up: climate, grass, cows, transatlantic trade, dogs, music, and the dairy and food-science faculty, peculiar in Ireland to UCC, are all part of this intertwined complex which is Cork city.

The cow and the Butter Exchange, are the inland symbols for the city; the official chartered symbol, however, is a ship, sailing safely into harbour between two castles: a symbol of security and adventure. At the head of navigation, Cork as a port city is a gateway to faraway places and peoples. The city arms also symbolise the role of the outsider in shaping the city: symbolise its functions as a controlling centre for the colonist, with its garrisons and naval fleets. It was a cosmopolitan place in the eighteenth century, with a great variety of peoples and churches. This new colonial city also had a triangular commercial structure: the old traditional shopping streets of the medieval core; the upmarket and more 'cosmopolitan' Patrick Street; and the financial and professional quarters of the linear South Mall. This latter zone is now owned, to a considerable extent, by international companies and financiers and is geared to their needs. Cork Corporation still tries to retain the vitality of these inner city places which now must compete with the burgeoning suburban shopping centres. So after a century of relative stagnation, the outside world now impinges deeply upon this city, with its airport and oil depots, and its satellite towns working in the new industrial estate of Little Island and elsewhere. The state's role is symbolised in the outer harbour, where a number of industries fluctuate in the storms generated by a new international division of labour and, above all, by a new, mainly American-centered technocratic consciousness. This consciousness is assisted by imported media forms which hammer home the message that technology and science can solve *all* our problems, not least those of unemployment. Cork's vulnerability, like Ireland's vulnerability, is shown by the effects of decisions in Detroit or wherever, which reverberate with often devastating effects on the homes of people scattered across the city, in some streets in Blackrock, Garrán na mBráthar, Fearann Rí and Blarney Street — indeed in every community in the city. There are many hidden Irelands here; and much pain.[21]

One last image of Cork: a trainload of government ministers and senior civil servants who travel south to visit the remote provincial centre where the great industries have closed, inspected the situation, interviewed the locals (who, as a minister once put it, spoke a dialect as fascinating and inscrutable as Chinese), and then returned to the metropolis — the Joycean centre of paralysis. Then the political impotence, the peripherality and marginality of this so-called regional capital struck home: an impotence which is only matched by the wit and humanity of the city, even in its adversity.

We have looked at three different kinds of settlements, which exemplify some important aspects of place in Ireland. I now want to look briefly at the role of capital cities and especially Dublin. James Joyce, that marvellous geographer, has recorded the Dublin world in detail, and made it into a universal symbol, creating a modern vision of urban man's life experience.[22] We can take for granted, then, I hope, Dublin's internal human geographies: a city stuffed full of a thousand villages, each with their own variety, richness and pain.[23] Our concern here is how Dublin governs itself and other places in the rest of the country.

For almost a millenium, Dublin has been the great broker between most of Ireland and the rest of the world. For much of that time, Dublin has performed as a masterful 'colonial' city, a fulcrum in the transmission of goods and peoples into the regions and localities, translating and dispatching directives from the metropolitan core in London. And even in the period when the new state strove for greater self-sufficiency, Dublin's centralising functions grew disproportionately. Today, Dublin mediates the bewildering variety of incentives and regulations that emanate from the Tower of Berlaymont in Brussels. Unlike Cork, for example, where the church-spires hold at least some, if not too much, of the high ground, the iconography of the Dublin skyline is now dominated by the headquarters of banks, insurance firms, trade unions, government departments, semi-state bodies, advertising agencies and a host of other media institutions — including Radio Telefís Éireann — which now dominate Irish society. [24]

Barrington has been the most eloquent of the critics who have challenged the economic, political and administrative rationale for retaining this highly centralised top-down management of this society. [25] The sense of alienation from and dissatisfaction with the central authority is now a wider global phenomenon; but it seems particularly acute in Ireland. To know who you are as a people is vital to the balance of all our lives, and the picture now appears to be one of enormous imbalance — the cult of linear progress and technocratic rule is literally bulldozing so much of our rural and urban heritage and in the process eliminating part of our memory, part of our identity, part of our future. Over-centralisation is another consequence, from schools through cooperatives and hospitals to government offices generally. As Paddy Duffy has noted in relation to rural planning the abstract bureaucratic view does not perceive rural areas as separate and precious entities; [26] and there is little, if any, appreciation in Dublin or Brussels of regional and local variations in levels of rurality or urbanity.

And yet, as in many other parts of the world, there are signs of counter-thrusts against these levelling forces. The great challenge is to combine a necessary balance between openness and enclosure, between adventure and security, between reaching out to the universal world and creating an identifiable home. The inland pull, the introverted drive — snaking inwards like the scrolls of Celtic art — still retains its essential powers in the rural areas. But, as we have seen, all Irish places are interwoven layers of many cultural elements. Here, on the edge of Europe, some of these layers lie exposed. The fault-lines still collide; the wounds still lie open. In Belfast today the rawness of the wounds has made the military elite, the planners, and indeed the often frightened communities, combine to opt for inner-city residential designs which only emphasise enclosure, defence, exclusion: [27] in a line from John Montague's *The Rough Field*:

> hatreds sealed into
> a hygienic honeycomb. [28]

The south has still more time and leisure to explore its own consciousness, and to recognise the plurality of places and experiences that make up this island. In the process, it can challenge the crippling assumptions of both older, introverted myths, and some global ones as well, which now sees Mercator's rule superseded by satellite and coastal surveillance. The sovereignty of the skies of smaller countries now seems a thing of the past. The challenge of the maritime frontier remains. But above all the challenge is to make more central the values of smaller places, not just Ireland and within Ireland, but smaller countries and places the world over. Top-down decentralisation can only touch the externals of local and regional life: real decentralisation calls for an effort to revitalize the creative energies of peoples, in caring for their own streets, localities and regions. The relocation of the artist, and the humanities generally to the centre of Irish life is necessary to this endeavour. The balance between the male and female ethos needs also to be restored; and in this context, the 'femaleness' of reflective and intuitive traditions (pre-Christian, Christian and non-Christian) are still available for creative exploration.[31] The richness and diversity of Irish musical expressions also point to some of the possibilities of openness.[32] Part of this vision also involves the recognition of the fragility and limited nature of the earth's resources.

All of this suggests a liberating redefinition of who we are; for sureness of identity is a necessary defence against the forces of cultural standardisation. Politically, surely it is not a question of deciding between the two great imperialisms of this age; nor simply one of adopting a standoff neutral position: but stating positively what it means to be a many-sided post-colonial society, and so reaching out to so much of the world that has endured rather than ruled.

> We shall not cease from exploration
> and the end of all our exploring
> will be to arrive where we started
> and know the place for the first
> time.[33]

T.S. Eliot is here expressing the central importance of self-knowledge in human experience. Knowing ourselves, and knowing our place for the first time, is the best starting-point from which to try to forge a better place between the wilderness and the eternal city.

NOTES AND REFERENCES

1.
> To lift the lid of peat
> and find this pupil dreaming
> of neolithic wheat!
> When he stripped off blanket bog
> The soft-piled centuries

> Fell open like a glib:
> There were the first plough-marks,
> The stone-age fields, the tomb
> Corbelled, turfed and chambered,
> Floored with dry turf-coomb.

Here Seamus Heaney in his poem 'Belderg' from *North* (London, 1975) stresses the richness of the Irish heritage that lies buried beneath the bogs. The geographer who has contributed most to lifting back 'the lid of peat' to reveal the many worlds beneath is E. Estyn Evans whose book *The Personality of Ireland* (2nd ed., Belfast, 1981) highlights the subtle depth and complexity of Irish culture and landscapes as revealed in the oral as compared with the official documented sources. New breakthroughs in research-techniques (as in palaeoecology and underwater archaeology) applied to our lakes, coasts and bogs will likely reveal even richer and more complex cultural substratums over the next decade.

2. Seamus Deane has reminded us [*Crane Bag*, (8)1, 1984, 90] that it was Yeats who once said that 'Ireland belonged to Asia until the battle of the Boyne'. Here Yeats was stressing, in a characteristic vivid phrase, both Ireland's position at the extreme western end of the old Indo-European world and Ireland's capacity, like India, for example, to achieve early cultural unity in the context of highly fragmented political structures. He may also be referring to the social structures of traditional Ireland, dominated as they were by aristocratic and learned castes and underpinned by a powerful peasant culture. Yeats may also be referring to the Irish view of the Cosmos in which time is seen as cyclical and eternal and in which man and woman are balanced between the vivid realities of Heaven and the Underworld. Some issues of the *Crane Bag* have explored further the implications of Ireland's peripheral Indo-European position: see, in particular, P. MacCana 'Notes on the early Irish concept of unity', The *Crane Bag*, 2, (1/2), 1978, 57-71.

3. C. Ó Loingsigh, *Pathways in history*, I, The Educational Company of Ireland, Dublin, 1983.

4. Geographers and cartographers have therefore been long involved in staking out new lands for princes and merchants and designing new territorial frameworks for the management of such colonies. Preston James in *All possible worlds: a history of geographical ideas* (New York, 1981) explores this theme in some depth.

5. Likewise, the nineteenth century Ordnance Survey six-inch maps, and their associated land-valuation records, provide a bureaucrat's list of every Irish name, and the content of every territory and every house in the island. Brian Friel's play *Translations* (London 1981) captures the intrusive nature of such a

mapping venture in Donegal, dealing here with both the trauma of language change — of *speaking* English but still *living* Irish — and the eternal problems of authority and alienation.

The intimate scale of the six-inch map, however, indicates a kind of cartographic half-way house between the imperial mapmaker, usually working on a grand scale and the local Irish surveyor concerned essentially with precise measurements of tiny pieces of land

> . . . . who owned
> that half a rood of rock, a no-man's land
> surrounded by our pitchfork-armed claims
>
> (P. Kavanagh, 'Epic', *Collected Poems*, London, 1964)

The Ordnance Survey six-inch map is therefore a hybrid — a compromise between two mapping traditions (and cultures) and so can also be used as a bridge — as a translation agency — into local geographies and other ways of viewing the world. See also 'Translations and a Paper Landscape: Between fiction and history', Brian Friel, John Andrews and Kevin Barry, The *Crane Bag*, 7 (2), 1983, 118-124, and P.A. Ferguson 'Irish map history: a select bibliography of secondary works 1850-1983', *Tenth International Conference on the history of Cartography*, Dublin, 1983, for a detailed listing, amongst other things, of the rich corpus of works on Irish maps and mapping by Professor John Andrews.

6. See, for example, W.J. Smyth, 'Property, patronage and population — reconstructing the human geography of mid-seventeenth century Tipperary', chapter in *Tipperary essays* (ed.), W. Nolan, forthcoming, Dublin, 1985, for an elucidation of seventeenth century transformations and continuities; and for an analysis of the landlord's impact in the same county see Willie Nolan's chapter in the same volume and 'Estate records and the making of the Irish landscape: a case-study from Co. Tipperary', *Irish Geography*, 9, 1976, 29-49.

7. Introductory texts in cultural geography include P.L. Wagner and M.W. Mikesell (eds), *Readings in cultural geography*, Chicago, 1962 and P.L. Wagner, *Environments and peoples*, Englewood Cliffs, 1972. One of the most stimulating papers in this field is D.E. Sopher's 'Place and location: notes on the spatial patterning of culture; chapter in *The idea of culture in the social sciences*, L. Schneider and C. Bonjean (eds.), Cambridge U.P., 1973. There is also a growing literature in geography on 'A sense of place'. See Yi Fu Tuan, *Topophilia,* Englewood Cliffs, 1974 and *Space and place*, London, 1977 and also E. Relph, *Place and placelessness,* London, 1976. For poetic perspectives on this latter theme in Ireland see Seamus Heaney, 'The sense of place' in *Preoccupations: selected prose 1968-1978*, London, 1980 and John Montague, *The dead kingdom*, Mountrath-Portlaoise, 1984.

8. For the general development of key ideas in this area in geography see D. Gregory, *Ideology, science and human geography*, London, 1978 and for a more detailed elaboration of this perspective in Irish geography, see W.J. Smyth, 'Social geography of rural Ireland: inventory and prospect', chapter 12 in the *Irish Geography Jubilee Volume*, Dublin 1984. This latter volume celebrates the 50th anniversary of the foundation of the Geographical Society of Ireland and comprises a 15 chapter review of major developments in each subfield of the discipline in Ireland.

9.   K. Whelan, 'The Catholic parish, the Catholic chapel and village development in Ireland', *Irish Geography*, 16, 1983, 1-16.

10. Tom Jones Hughes, Professor of Geography at University College Dublin, has inspired a whole generation of younger Irish geographers in this and related areas of Ireland's historical and social geography. See, for example, his 'Historical geography of Ireland from *circa* 1700', Chapter 9 in *Irish Geography Jubilee Volume, op. cit.,* 149-166.

11. These points are more fully developed in W.J. Smyth, 'Continuity and change in the territorial organisation of Irish rural communities', Part I, *Maynooth Review*, 1(1), 1975, 51-73.

12. See, in particular, F. Barth, *Ethnic groups and boundaries,* London, 1969, for an elaboration on these aspects. In the Irish context, see, for example, Gearóid Ó Crualaioch 'The primacy of form; a 'Folk Ideology' in de Valera's politics' (*De Valera and his times, (*eds.), J.P. O'Carroll and J.A. Murphy) where he observes that a national ideology was built on 'an essentially static conception of a "truly Irish" way of life, a static conception that derives from both the eighteenth century Romantic roots of Davis's vision and also older and perennial, native, Gaelic roots involving the personification of Irish sovereignty in a mother figure who must be delivered from bondage . . .' (49).

13. W.J. Smyth, *Maynooth Review, op. cit.,* 1/2, Part II, 1975, 152-201 and also Thomas Davis lecture 'The cultural geography of rural Ireland in the twentieth century', W. Nolan (ed.), *Ireland: the geographical dynamic,* forthcoming, Cork, 1985.

14. County Tipperary has been defined by historical and cultural geographers as belonging to a wider culture region which embraces East-Munster and South-Leinster and also curves north along the Barrow to include the Old Pale region in Leinster. This is a cultural region, it could be argued, where the long-established interaction between Normans and Gaels produced a new rich hybrid culture which was well-accustomed to dealing with and living in an urban commercial economy and which was in consequence stratified into clear class groupings including for example, a very significant landless labourer and cottier class. It may well have been the networks of middle-class alliances between town and country in this region which produced many of the more sophisticated agrarian/anti-tithe movements, which certainly provided both the patronage and personnel for the reconstruction of the modern Catholic Church, including the provision of both leaders and locales for the indigenous religious orders, the Christian Brothers and the Presentation Sisters. It was also this region which provided the leadership and organisational structures to launch and sustain the Cooperative movement, farming organisations like the National Farmers Association and Macra na Feirme, parish self-help movements like Muintir na Tíre not to speak of the colossus of the Gaelic Athletic Association. Tipperary could therefore be described as belonging to a wider region which has often utilised radical political strategies to achieve the conservative goals of maintaining, sustaining or reviving what its elites felt were the most central elements in their 'cultural' heritage. It should also be noted, however, that this region also produced some of the most powerful cottier/small-farmer/artisan alliances and

agrarian societies which were often in conflict with the eventually victorious middle-class forces in the society.

15. The diversity of place-biographies in Co. Tipperary — particularly those of its minority Protestant communities — are more fully developed in 'The cultural geography of rural Ireland in the twentieth century', *op. cit.*

16. Kevin Whelan in his chapter 'The Catholic Church in County Tipperary 1700-1900' in *Tipperary essays, op. cit.* details the elaborate iconography of this Cathedral town, drawing attention in particular to specific details of the impressive statue to Archbishop Croke and the 1798 monument, both on Liberty Square, and the Archbishop Leahy statue and the Marian grotto across the bridge to the east in the extensive ecclesiastical sector of the town.

17. I.D.A. Promotional publications Cork: See B.M. Brunt 'Manufacturing changes in the Greater Cork Area 1980-84', *Irish Geography*, 17, 1984, 101-107 for detailed analysis of new industrial developments in the region.

18. Sean Beecher's *A dictionary of Cork slang* (Cork, 1983) which explores the distinctive 'patois of the native Corkonian', reveals the rich, colourful and uninhibited language of older parts in the city. Cork-born Seán Ó Faoláin in *An Irish journey* (London, 1940) describes his own native city (pp. 75-93) noting that 'It is one of those towns you love and hate. Some wag said that in Cork you do not commit sin; you achieve it. You do not, likewise, enjoy life in Cork; you experience it. For it is a town with a sting, inhabited by the Irish Gascons, the most acidulous race we breed, the most alive, the keenest, sharpest and toughest . . .' The classic geographical introduction to the nature of places in cities as perceived and experienced by their inhabitants is K. Lynch, *The image of the city,* Cambridge, Mass, 1960.

19. For detailed scholarly analysis of these worlds, see J.K. Hourihan, 'Residential satisfaction, neighbourhood attributes, and personal characteristics: an exploratory path analysis in Cork, Ireland'. *Environment and Planning A*, Vol. 16, 1984, pp. 425-436 and 'Context-Dependent models of residential satisfaction: an analysis of housing groups in Cork, Ireland' *Environment and Behavior,* Vol. 16, 1984, pp. 369-393; Ellen M. Mackey, 'A factorial ecology of Cork City', M.A. Dissertation, Department of Social Theory and Institutions, University College Cork.

20. Michael Gough, 'A history of the physical development of Cork City' M.A. dissertation, Department of Geography, University College Cork, 1974; Angela Fahy, 'The spatial differentiation of commercial and residential functions in Cork city 1787-1863', *Irish Geography,* 17, 1984, 17-26.

21. We have as yet to explore the cultural geography of these old and new housing estates — indeed the geography of life in the backstreets and new council estates of Clogheen, Thurles, Cork or wherever has yet to be written. Much of the life of the middle-class suburb is also hidden. Indeed, there are at least two kinds of human geographies to such places. First, a *daytime* geography when the generally male householders commute to the city to work, the children go to school and the housewives shape their world with its own rhythms, pains and solidarities and second, a *nighttime* geography of domestic and other encounters which have never been explored or mapped. To capture the real geography of these places, one would need to be able to embrace all the

conversations and exchanges, in both domestic and public arenas, which interlock and reverberate across this still closely-knit city. And a striking feature of that nighttime geography is the bulge of the younger generation seeking to create their own worlds and meeting-places in the city, not just jostling for places in schools, factories and offices but also encroaching upon and colonising the formerly sedate public houses of the older 'regulars' who dominated in a more stagnant era. There are also distinctive cultural geographies of the elderly and the inner city poor generally, not to speak of the routines and stresses of the youngest married couples in the still expanding suburban frontiers on the edge of the city. Likewise, the city is now over-spilling into former rural parishes like Glounthaune. Here the contrasts are sharpest between the still vibrant chapel-communities of places like Knockraha and the high-walled, hedged and well-protected detached managerial houses off the Youghal Road and the more densely populated intimate worlds of the new public housing estates on Little Island. There are many new Irelands juxtaposed in this as in other metropolitan regions in the country with communities occupying the same physical space but not sharing the same world views or the same fields of activity and interaction.

22.   James Joyce, *Ulysses*, London, 1958.

23.   Geographers who have 'explored' Dublin include J.P. Haughton 'The social geography of Dublin', *Geographical Review*, 39, 1949, 257-77; J. Brady and A. J. Parker, 'The factorial ecology of Dublin: a preliminary investigation', *Economic and Social Review* 6 (3), 1975, 35-54; J.K. Hourihan, 'Social areas in Dublin', *Economic and Social Review*, 9, 1978, 310-18 and M.J. Bannon, J.G. Eustace and M. O'Neill, *Urbanisation: problems of growth and decay in Dublin*. N.E.S.C. Report 55; Dublin, 1981.

24.   Apart from its central organising role within the state, Dublin was and is most exposed to outside economic and cultural influences given its dominant link role with other national capitals and cultures. Dublin, therefore, has been and is the major diffusion centre for secularising trends and other world views which arise from the increasing integration of the culture of western capital cities on the one hand and the related growth of cultural distances as between such international metropolitan regions and other regions within the countries concerned. And as Michael Bannon has consistently argued, unless Government policy in relation to the office/service sector changes, Dublin's unique advantages 'as a capital city and as a centre for research and knowledge may serve to intensify rather than diminish concentration' (M.J. Bannon 'The Irish national settlement system' in *Urbanisation and settlement systems* [eds.] L.S. Bourne, R. Sinclair and K. Dzienwonski, Oxford U.P., 1983). In terms of 'media geographies', an interesting point here is the relative proportion of 'outsider/broker/insider' contributions to flows of information etc. In this respect the percentage figures in multi-channel T.V. areas, for example, which suggest that — at peak viewing times — for every one house watching RTE 1 programmes, there may be ten tuned into either the BBC or ITV is instructive (*Aspect*, November, 1984). Thus the powerful role of new medias for 'tribalising' or 'retribalising' societies should not be underestimated and in this context the battles for the control of local radio and other medias highlights not only their potential for profits but

also their perceived significance in shaping the nature and values of society both in the short and the long run.

25.   T.J. Barrington, *The Irish administrative system,* Dublin, 1980; and 'What happened to Irish Government' in F. Litton (ed.), *Unequal achievement; the Irish experience 1957-72,* Dublin, 1982. For another perspective on this question, see D. Fennell, *The state of the Nation: Ireland since the sixties,* Dublin, 1983.

26.   P.J. Duffy, 'Rural settlement change in the Republic of Ireland — a preliminary discussion', *Geoforum,* 14(2), 1983, 185-191. See also his essay and other essays in *Change and development in rural Ireland,* G.S.I. Conference, Maynooth College, 20 October 1984.

27.   G.M. Dawson, 'Defensive planning in Belfast', *Irish Geography,* 17, 1984, 27-41. On the wider questions of ethnicity and segregation in Belfast, see also the numerous works of Fred Boal, including 'Segregation and mixing — space and residence in Belfast' in F.W. Boal and J.N.H. Douglas (eds.), *Integration and division: geographical perspectives on the Northern Ireland problem,* London, 1982.

28.   J. Montague, *The rough field,* Dublin, 1972.

29.   See, for example, J. Gottmann, *The significance of territory.* Charlottesville, 1973, 123-160; A. Buttimer, 'Grasping the dynamism of lifeworld', *Annals Association of American Geographers,* 66, (2), 1976. T. Hägerstrand, 'Survival and arena: on the life-history of individuals in relation to their geographical environment' in T. Carlstein, D. Parkes and N. Thrift (eds.), *Human activity and time geography,* Vol. 2, London, 1978, 122-145.

30.   Given the revolutionary nature and speed of technological economic, social and cultural changes now taking place, it could be argued that the whole arena of *adult* and continuing education should occupy a far more central position in our educational priorities.

31.   See, for example, The *Crane Bag,* 4 (1), 1980, *Images of the Irish Woman,* including P. MacCana, 'Women in Irish mythology'; 7-11 and N. O'Connor, 'Human encounter: beyond the philosophy of male and female', 20-26.

32.   Micheál Ó Súilleabháin provides a stimulating and liberating outline of the complex history of, current trends in, and new possibilities and creativities of the Irish musical scene, The *Crane Bag,* 5 (2), 1981.

33.   T.S. Eliot, 'Little Gidding' in *Four Quartets,* London, 1979, 48.

ACKNOWLEDGEMENTS

Many people have helped to shape the ideas embedded in this paper but I owe a very special debt to Karin, Éamonn and Mary for ensuring that the text finally saw the light of day.

Stability and Ambivalence: aspects of the sense of Place and Religion in Irish Literature

At the beginning of this century a little-known poet, Pádraig Ó hÉigeartaigh, writing in the United States of the drowning of his son Donncha, laments his young child being buried under a hostile sod:

> Ochón! a Dhonncha, mo mhíle cogarach, fén
>   bhfód so sínte;
> fód an doichill 'na luí ar do cholainn bhig,
>   mo loma-sceimhle!
> Dá mbeadh an codladh so i gCill na Dromad ort nó
>   in uaigh san Iarthar
> mo bhrón do bhogfadh, cé gur mhór mo dhochar, is
>   ní bheinn id' dhiaidh air.

In Thomas Kinsella's version:

> My sorrow, Donncha, my thousand-cherished under
>   this sod stretched,
> this mean sod lying on your little body —
>   my utter fright . . . .
> If this sleep were on you in Cill na Dromad
>   or some grave in the West
> it would ease my sorrow, though great the
>   affliction and I'd not complain.[1]

Few Irish people will question the poet's notion of the foreign soil being mean or hostile. Neither will very many wonder unduly about the whereabouts of Cill na Dromad. Indeed it scarcely matters *where* it is, because we all know *what* it is: the centre of one's universe, the beloved home-place/parish/territory.

One will probably find a reverential feeling for home-place in every country throughout the world, but it is unlikely that it is to be found so deeply rooted in any West European culture, at any rate, as it is in Irish culture. It seems to have made its presence felt in Irish literature at every level and in every era from early historic times to the present day.

The idea of an Irish city or town being the loved home-place is, one feels, of fairly recent origin. Not, perhaps, until James Joyce wrote Ulysses did a whole Irish city figure unreservedly in serious literature as one man's revered universe. Seán O'Casey and Brendan Behan are amongst those who have since added significantly to the sense of Dublin city as home. Some of the various small communities in other Irish cities, such as Cork, have been lovingly explored in novels and short stories, but one doubts if the centrality of the city itself in the mind and feeling of its inhabitants has been established in any of these works. Indeed Cork figures as quite an unbeloved place in a major work from the twelfth century, The Vision of Mac Conglinne.[2] In this splendid piece of satire, the monastic city of Cork is seen as a place to be avoided, a place of petty restrictions, verminous lodgings, and ecclesiastics who wield with great effect their croziers, and where the River Lee is an instrument of torture. But, by and large, the places revered and identified with in traditional Irish literature are rural places — the townland of Cill na Dromad rather than the town of Killarney, the parish of Iveleary rather than the city of Cork. And while over half of the population of the Republic lives today in cities and large towns, it appears that considerable numbers of our urban dwellers still look to the ancient rural home-place. Máirtín Ó Direáin, amongst modern poets, is a classic case: much of his work centres on his feeling of being an exile, uprooted in 'the deceitful city'.[3] Even Séamas Heaney in his most recent volume is found speaking of the threat of 'the empty city'.[4] The multitudes of people of rural origins who have helped, however passively, to make Joyce's Dublin a wasteland — and who flee it at weekends for a more congenial life in the country — are probably making their own quite complicated comment.

Cities and towns — particularly on the east coast — have historically been the creations and preserves of invading colonists, and the consequent sense of alienation of the native population may help to explain some of the difficulty many Irish people still have in identifying fully with urban life. The main reason for this difficulty, however, must stem from the special decentralised and rural nature of Irish society itself from pre-historic times down to the recent past. Eoin Mac Neill has said: 'We find the ancient Greeks organised like the Irish in small political communities, but these [Greek communities] . . . are based in each case on a walled town. The Irish state remained a rural city, a city of the fields.'[5] The land of Ireland in pre-Elizabethan times was divided into anything from one hundred to two hundred of such 'rural cities', all autonomous or semi-autonomous kingdoms. The chieftain-kings of these territories — and often, doubtless, the sub-chieftains of even smaller territories — were imagined from ancient times as being wedded to their land. Inauguration ceremonies of an archaic pre-Christian form, symbolising the nuptial ties between chieftain and place, were enacted down to the seventeenth century. Even in the late eighteenth century when Eibhlín Dhubh Ní Chonaill made her famous lament for her husband Art Ó Laoghaire it was clearly still the norm to think of the ancestral kingdom as blazing up in grief for the death of its aristocratic spouse.[6]

Generally speaking, families clearly identified with particular places did not move outside the territorial limits. And it is quite surprising, despite all our wars and plantations, how many of the descendants of our aristocratic families still live on to-day in the old beloved territories — the McCarthys and the O'Learys in their Cork territories, the O'Dohertys in Donegal, the O'Neills in Tyrone, the O'Byrnes in Wicklow, the O'Flahertys in Galway, the O'Donoghue's in Kerry . . . .

It seems then that it is the sacred wedding of territory to chief — and by extension of territory to kin — which is at the heart of the passion for place in Irish life and literature. Parallel with this bonding, of course, was the bonding of each free family group with its own particular inherited land. Down to our own day each field, hill and hillock was named with affection, while certain of these sites became famous because of the mythological or heroic memories associated with them. Wordsworth complained that England, unlike Greece, lacked hills or mountains 'by the celestial muses glorified'.[7] Ireland, like Greece, had scarce a hill or foot of land which was not invested in some way with historical or mythological glory.

All this was given special recognition in early medieval Ireland in the form of a branch of learning called *Dinnsheanchas*, the lore of high places. No poet was accounted educated if he was not fully acquainted with the *dinnsheanchas*. Place-names, as a consequence, became a part of the resonance of some of the finest literary works of the medieval age such as *Agallamh na Seanórach* (The Colloquoy of the Ancients), *Buile Shuibhne* (recently translated as *Sweeney Astray* by Seamus Heaney), and the lays and lyrics of the Fianna.

It cannot be entirely co-incidental that the lore of place emerged as a part of the early medieval tendency in Ireland to consolidate the primacy of the old pre-christian literature, and that some of the more notable *dinnsheanchas*-type literature — such as *Buile Shuibhne* — written down ironically enough in monasteries, is markedly anti-christian or anti-clerical in tone. Karl Popper has remarked that when a culture is under severe strain it either completely rejects existing society or looks for a Utopia in the past or in the future.[8] There is evidence to suggest that the deeply-rooted archaic Irish society, put under strain by the advent of Christianity, sought its Utopia in the old pagan past. There is at any rate a series of fine literary works from the ninth century *Hag of Beare* and the twelfth century *Buile Shuibhne* down to some of the later lays and lyrics of the Fianna in the 17th century which dramatises the longing of Irish people for the freedoms of the old pagan past, and these freedoms are commonly associated with famous places where mythological or heroic events took place. In the literature of the Fianna, which was being listened to with glee in our Gaeltachtaí right down into the twentieth century, Oisín son of Fionn keeps on persuading St. Patrick of the pre-eminence of the old pre-Christian life, and in doing so creates a litany of beloved place-names as an invocation of freedom and beauty:

> Sgolghaire Luin Doire an Chairn,
> búithre an daimh ó Aill na gCaor,
> ceol le gcodladh Fionn go moch,
> lachain ó Loch na dTrí gCaol.

> Throat-song of the blackbird of Doire an Chairn
>   and the stag's call from Aill na gCaor
> were Fionn's music, sleeping at morn,
>   and the ducks from Loch na dTrí gCaol,

> the grouse at Cruachan, seat of Conn,
>   otters whistling at Druim Dá Loch,
> eagle cry in Gleann na bhFuath,
>   cuckoos' murmur on Cnoc na Scoth,

> dogs' voices in Gleann Caoin,
>> cry of the half-blind hunting eagle,
> patter of hounds, on their way early
>> in from Tráigh na gCloch nDearg.
>
> When Fionn and the Fianna lived
>> they loved the hills, not hermit-cells.
> Blackbird speech is what they loved
> — not the sound, unlovely, of your bells.[9]

In all of this literature connected with place — even in the nature lyrics written by monks in the golden age of early Christianity — there is no sense of the mystic presence of God or Spirit such as one finds in the literature of other peoples. Rather one is continually struck with the feeling that place and natural phenomena connote above all stability, certainty, eternity on earth.

In more recent centuries the feeling for place has been acutely intensified by events following on the English conquest: plantations, evictions, enforced exile. There is scarcely one of the many hundreds of poets writing in Irish in the seventeenth, eighteenth, and nineteenth centuries whose poems do not focus in some way on his feeling for home or ancestral land; and some poems which have to do with the destruction of famous places, such as Kilcash, hover on the edge of heartbreak.

The traditional treatment of home-place and territory in literature survived in good measure the linguistic changeover in the nineteenth century from Irish to English. In the case, however, of a great number of English-language ballads of beloved places and counties, the maudlin often asserts itself. It seemed for a time that scarce an Irish tenor existed who did not harbour a sugar-coated Cill na Dromad in his fermenting heart . . . .

But the old values continue to be reflected with dignity and perception in the verse of poets such as Kavanagh, Montague, Kinsella, Heaney, and in prose-works such as Behan's *Borstal Boy*. There is no doubting, for instance, that place (with its special connotation of stability) fuels real passion in the poetry of Patrick Kavanagh. In his poem on the black hills of Shancoduff,[10] 'eternally' looking 'north towards Armagh', he clearly identifies the heart of his own universe:

> These are my Alps and I have climbed the Matterhorn
> With a sheaf of hay for three perishing calves
> In the field under the Big Forth of Rocksavage.

Séamas Heaney points to a certain lack of dimension in Kavanagh's use of place in his work. 'Kavanagh's place-names', he says, 'are there to stake out a personal landscape, they declare one man's experience, they are denuded of tribal or etymological implications. Mucker, Dundalk, Inniskeen, provide no *frisson* beyond the starkness of their own dunting, consonantal noises'.[11] It can be said then that while passion for place remains an integral part of the poetry of Patrick Kavanagh, sense of place — the sense of all the historical, mythological, ideological, familial associations I have been mentioning — tends to disappear. In the nineteenth century linguistic change-over the passion has been cut off to some extent from its primal Irish source, and remains somewhat under-developed, unarticulated.

On the other hand a modern poet writing in Irish such as Máirtín Ó Direáin has no difficulty in fitting his own long lyric obsession with the island of Aran into the complete traditional framework, while a much younger poet, Nuala Ní Dhomhnaill, has made unique creative use of her sense of place in some remarkable poems written on her return from Turkey to settle down in West Kerry. In one of these poems, *Baile an tSléibhe*[12] she identifies with the places and wild flora of her ancestral district, and moves easily in a short space from personal and family involvement to her awareness of the folklore and mythology associated with named places, such as the ancient (probably) aristocratic habitation of Cathair Léith in the townland of Baile an tSléibhe:

> I mBaile an tSléibhe
> tá Cathair Léith
> is laistíos dó
> tigh mhuintir Dhuinnshléibhe;
> as san chuaigh an file Seán
> 'on Oileán
> is uaidh sin tháinig an ghruaig rua
> is bua na filíochta
> anuas chugam
> trí cheithre ghlúin.
>
> Ar thaobh an bhóthair
> tá seidhleán
> folaithe ag crainn fiúise,
> is an feileastram
> buí

ó dheireadh mhí Aibreáin
go lár an Mheithimh,
is sa chlós tá boladh
lus anainne nó camán meall
mar a thugtar air sa dúiche
timpeall,
i gCill Uru is i gCom an Liaigh
i mBaile an Chóta is i gCathair Boilg.

Is lá
i gCathair Léith
do léim breac geal
ón abhainn
isteach sa bhuicéad
ar bhean
a chuaigh le ba
chun uisce ann,
an tráth
gur sheoil trí árthach
isteach sa chuan,
gur neadaigh an fiolar
i mbarr an chnoic
is go raibh laincisí síoda
faoi chaoire na Cathrach.

*   *   *

In Baile an tSléibhe
is Cathair Léith
and below it
the house of the Dunleavies;
from here the poet Seán
went into the Great Blasket
and from here the red hair
and gift of poetry came down to me
through four generations.

Beside the road
there is a stream
covered over with fuchsias
and the wild flag
yellow
from the end of April
to mid-June,

and in the yard there is a scent
of pineapple mayweed or camomile
as it is commonly known in the surrounding
countryside,
in Cill Uru and in Com an Liaigh
in Ballinchouta and in Cathairbuilig.

And one day
in Cathair Léith
a white trout leaped
out of the river
and into the bucket
of a woman
who had lead her cows
to water there;
a time
when three ships came sailing
into the bay
the eagle was still nesting
on the top of the hill
and the sheep of Cathair
had spancels of silk.

However one judges this poem — and I think myself it is a poem of
fine quality — it shows that a whole vast cultural and personal identification with rural place can still occur, particularly through the
mediation of the Irish language.

There is a sense in which place finally becomes co-extensive in the
mind, not only with personal and ancestral memories, but with the
whole living community culture. If one's day to day pattern of living
is found good, the feeling of identification with its place of origin is
accordingly enhanced. Community becomes place, place community. This is especially true of traditional Irish society which placed
such emphasis on regional or local autonomy, as well as on cooperative community living. The numerous communities of
medieval Ireland do not appear to have looked much to outside centres for cultural guidance — unlike England or France, for instance,
where similar regional communities might have looked to the central
courts of London or Paris to set the literary, political, intellectual,
and behavioural patterns. Chieftain-kings in each of our traditional
kingdoms were to a great extent self-sufficient and all maintained
various kinds of poets, musicians, historians, lawyers, storytellers. [13]

The influence of such retinues in small communities must have been one of the determining factors in establishing the flair for literary style, music, and storytelling inherited by people even in the most remote areas of Ireland today. This influence must also have been paramount in underpinning the whole cultural value-system of the people.

The value-systems of the various traditional regional communities throughout the country seem to have been quite similar. Very few expert anthropological or social studies have been carried out, however, to discover what these values were in the past, or to what extent they influence life or decisions to-day. For community leaders who would propose new departures in matters connected with our life-style, or who would wish to merge us more smoothly with the expanding 'European community', such knowledge would appear to be crucial.

I would hazard the guess that the main traditional value-system — as reflected primarily in Irish literature down to the nineteenth century — is still the dominant one in present day Ireland. It seems indeed likely that a people who would still identify so strongly with the age-old concept of place would also identify strongly with the whole range of community cultural values so inextricably linked with place. Some elements of this culture may be found somewhat distasteful, other elements highly acceptable; but distasteful or acceptable these are the elements our community leaders, from politicians to philosophers, have to deal with. They have to reckon above all with the inordinate self-fulfilment or (as some would say) the inordinate self-satisfaction our culture has always given us. . . .[14] Investigation of all this, of course, is properly a matter for social scientists.

I will refer briefly, however, to one salient feature of our traditional community culture — the religious dimension — about which there is abundant documentation in Irish literature, and which could be of particular relevance to present-day ethical controversies.

It has been rightly said that there is very little evidence for intellectual dissent or analysis, or indeed philosophic discourse, in the native Gaelic tradition. In different eras the chieftain-king, the poet, and finally the priest seems to have been the arbiter of what the doctrine or belief should be, and the community followed. Intellectual dissent emerges in substantial measure for the first time in the Anglo-Irish colony in Ireland in the work of Swift, Berkeley and others. The effect of Anglo-Irish dissent on Irish society was, however, of a very restricted nature.

But there is evidence of a deep dissent of another kind in traditional Irish literature. It is a dissent of the emotions which we have already seen openly expressed in regard to the imposition of Christianity in works such as the lays of the Fianna. The most common form of this dissent, however, is ambivalence or half-belief. Johan Huizanga in his book *Homo Ludens* declares that primitive man only half-believes in his own rituals: 'Their belief in the sanctities is a sort of half-belief', he says, 'and goes with scoffing and pretended indifference'.[15] Such half-belief has always existed, I believe, as a necessary condition of survival, not alone in primitive societies but in all deeply-rooted communities. Liberal intellectuals, floating free of community ties, do not always appreciate why members of deeply-rooted communities are very reluctant to change their received dogmas — dogmas in which, quite often, they only half-believe. This reluctance is to be attributed, I think, to an intuitive understanding that while some simple acceptable dogmas are necessary for ordering human affairs, a deep reservation exists always about the ability of any dogma — including liberal dogmas — to give satisfactory answers to the basic questions concerning life and death.

Whatever of that, an acquaintance with literature in Irish makes one extremely doubtful about whether traditional Irish society can be described in any clear sense as Catholic, or Christian. Unreserved identification with Christian values is more the exception than the rule. One does, of course, at most periods find a small elitist group of literary people — often clerics — who are quite obviously deeply devoted to Christian or Catholic ethics and doctrine. One also finds, as in the seventeenth century, the readiness of Irish people to claim the title Catholic to distinguish them from the invading Protestant. But the main body of Irish literature operates as if only superficially touched by Christianity. While ritualistic references to God or Christ abound, the value-system guiding the poets' feelings, from earliest historic times down to the nineteenth century, remains obdurately pre-Christian. One way of validating this view-point is to investigate the admired virtues in the vast body of eulogy or elegy written for patrons by their poets. One finds these virtues for the great part to be those of the heroic pre-Christian past. Even an eighteenth century poet such as O'Rahilly, who rails against the anti-Catholic laws of the

British parliament, rarely thinks of imputing Christian virtues —
such as belief in the sacredness of human life, or belief in a spiritual
after-life — to those he has admired. Rather he praises them for their
addiction to violence, to blood-letting, to revenge, or for their fatal
attraction to women. O'Rahilly himself on his death-bed has no
thought of an afterlife with a merciful God: he thinks only of an
afterlife under the earth with his fierce ancestral patrons, the
McCarthys:

> I will stop now — my death is hurrying near
> now the dragons of the Leamhan, Loch Léin and the
>   Laoi are destroyed.
> In the grave with this cherished chief I'll join
>   those kings
> my people served before the death of Christ.[16]

Similarly all our popular keens bear little evidence of emanating
from a Christian society. Eibhlín Dhubh Ní Chonaill, in the greatest
of these keens, sees the body of her husband Art in its final state as
merely bearing 'clay and stones': there is no sense of a consoling God
in this poem, no sense of re-union after death, no hope at all.[17]

Then again in our love-literature, from the sagas of early Ireland
through the learned literary lyrics of the Middle Ages down to the
folksong still being sung in our Gaeltachtaí, Christian values such as
the sanctity of marriage or the necessity of chastity get short shrift.
There is no sense of sexual sin in most of this literature. Indeed on a
few occasions when the thought of sin occurs it is directly challenged,
as when a folk poet says:

> Ní chreidim go bráth ó shagart nó ó bhráthair
> go bhfuil peaca ins an pháirt a dhúbladh.
>
> No priest or friar will I believe
> that it's sin to couple in love.[18]

It is widely accepted now, due to the work of historians such as Fr.
Canice Mooney, that down to the seventeenth century at any rate the
views held of sex and marriage by aristocrats, ecclesiastics and men
of learning were, to say the least of it, remarkably at variance with the
orthodox Catholic views. Indeed even Fr. Mooney, having explored
the histories of deviant aristocrats and bishops in the fourteenth, fif-
teenth, and sixteenth centuries, professes himself a little puzzled at

the fact than an ecclesiastic, one Cathal Óg Maguire, the son of a bishop, father of some dozen children (one of whom in turn married another bishop's daughter) was described in the Annals of Ulster after his death as 'a gem of purity and a turtle-dove of chastity'.[19] On reflection this seems more like invincible innocence than thoroughgoing ambivalence.

From the 17th century onwards stern efforts were made by a small band of Catholic clergy (aided by British legal measures) to introduce the Post-Tridentine reforms into the various districts of the country. Judging by the main body of literature in Irish these efforts had very limited success; but that some gains were made is evidenced by the work of a few religious poets and by the corpus of devotional prayers and stories which survived in folk memory. Not until the 19th century were the dogmas and devotions, now imagined to be the essence of traditional Irish Catholicism, propagated successfully. This new amalgam of Post-Tridentine Catholicism and British Victorianism, perpetuated as part of the language-change by the British educational system, made its greatest impact in cities and English-speaking areas. Large areas of rural Ireland, however, seem to have preserved meticulously their traditional ambivalence. . . . To read of the early nineteenth century living patterns in the County Kilkenny area as described in the diary of Amhlaoibh Ó Súilleabháin,[20] or in the County Tyrone area as described by Carleton — or indeed to read of the twentieth century living patterns in West Kerry as described in the writings of Pádraig Ó Maoileoin[21] is to be convinced of that.

On the other hand, James Joyce, citizen of east coast Dublin, was heavily burdened during his schooldays with the dogmatic Victorian version of Catholicism. His considered reaction was 'non serviam' — in effect the answer of Oisín to Saint Patrick in the late medieval lays of the Fianna. While there is a possibility that Joyce also may have been ambivalent for a time in regard to belief in some form of the supernatural, there is no question but that he finally found psychological stability in identifying only with the cities, rivers, and eternal 'high places' of this world, rather than of the next; with Dublin rather than with God. In all this his values are much closer to those of the central Irish tradition than has generally been supposed. Of course he developed these values spectacularly in a new urban environment. And, in so doing, he incidentally invites us to think of the possibility that we Irish could learn to live graciously in cities, and even grow to love them much as we loved the old rural home-places.

NOTES

1. Ó Tuama and Kinsella, *An Duanaire,* Poems of the Dispossessed, No. 68.
2. For an English version see Cross and Slover, *Ancient Irish Tales*, p. 551.
3. *Selected Poems/Tacar Dánta*, 1984, p. 75.
4. *Station Island*, 1984, p. 37.
5. *Early Irish Laws and Institutions*, 1935, pp. 99-100.
6. *An Duanaire*, p. 213.
7. *Poetical works* ed. T. Hutchinson, 1974; Miscellaneous Sonnets, No. V, p. 200.
8. Bryan Magee, *Popper*, Fontana, p. 89.
9. *An Duanaire*, No. 18.
10. *Collected Poems*, Martin Brian and O'Keefe, p. 30.
11. *Preoccupations*, 1980, p. 140.
12. *An Dealg Droighin*, 1981, p. 79.
13. All such professionals shared, of course, — and promoted — a common national view of Irish culture.
14. Writing of early Irish religious literature, James Carney says: "Most of us have heard the humorous verse: 'How odd/of God/to choose/the Jews'. But if the early Irish had questioned the ways of providence they would rather have asked: 'How did God fail/to choose the Gael'." (*Early Irish Poetry*, ed. J. Carney, p. 50).
15. P. 42, Paladin, 1970.
16. *An Duanaire*, No. 53.
17. *An Duanaire*, No. 62.
18. *An Duanaire*, No. 73.
19. *The Church in Gaelic Ireland* (13th to 15th centuries), pp. 58-60.
20. *Cinn-Lae Amhlaoibh Uí Shúileabháin*, edited and translated by Rev. M. Mac Craith, I.T.S. (four volumes).
21. See, in particular, *Na hAird ó Thuaidh* (1960) and *Bríde Bhán* (1968).

A Sense of Identity in the Irish Legal System

Introduction

In 1969 Mrs. Josie Airey was having marital problems and wished to obtain a judicial separation from her husband. The legal costs of separation proceedings in the High Court were prohibitive and Irish law did not give her the right to legal aid in such a case. Josie Airey was a woman of stern resolve, however, and in spite of enormous legal obstacles she succeeded some ten years later in getting a judgment from the Court of Human Rights in Strasbourg to the effect that the Irish Government was in breach of its obligations under the European Convention on Human Rights.[1] It was a case where an individual, a woman, took on the State and in the end, by appealing to an *external* forum, succeeded in getting the State to change its position on legal aid. The case illustrates vividly many points which I wish to make here tonight.

In my talk, I take as my point of departure the year 1960 because it was in or about this time that Irish lawyers began to fully realise for the first time that Bunreacht na hÉireann was a *legal* document. Up until then there was the feeling that the Constitution was merely an important statement of political aspiration and social doctrine. In the areas of fundamental rights especially there was a failure, by practicing lawyers at least, to fully appreciate that the Constitution created the framework for the State, indicated the limits of the State's powers and set out the fundamental rights of the individual. Once lawyers began to appreciate the *legal* significance of the document in relation to fundamental rights, however, once they discovered the potential of the Constitution, as it were, a veritable revolution occurred in the legal system. A revolution, which it may be said, had consequences not only for constitutional law, but also for other areas of public law and indeed for private law as well.[2]

What, it may be asked, occurred in the 'sixties which caused Irish lawyers to adopt this new perspective on the Constitution?

Well, for one thing, there was a dramatic improvement in legal education in the country. In 1963, for example, when I finished my legal studies in Dublin, the Law School in U.C.D., the biggest in the country did not have any *full-time* law teacher. Now there are more than 30 full-time law teachers in the Universities throughout the country. These new and young academics have brought a new professionalism to the law schools. There has been an increase in postgraduate studies and in research. The better students began to pursue their courses abroad. Many went to the U.S.A. where the financial assistance was greatest. The American legal connection was established. And for reasons I will explain later there was a shift away from the Common Law or the English approach.

Legal academic writing also increased. Again it is worth remarking that in the early 'sixties none of the main-stream subjects in law school had modern Irish textbooks. In the past twenty years things have changed impressively. We now have upwards of 30 Irish legal texts in all the main subject areas. All of this study and research into Irish Law led to the realisation that we *are* different here and that we have our own legal system. Irish lawyers became more confident, more self-reliant. In a sense, Irish lawyers came of age.

So what we have here now is a *younger,* a more *aggressive* breed of *full-time academics* writing about *Irish Law* increasingly suspicious of the inevitability of English solutions and willing to embrace more ardently the American and, (to a lesser extent), the continental experience. The law schools are also producing a *better educated law graduate* who in turn is willing to put novel arguments to the Courts. All of this is bound eventually to have a significant impact for the legal system.

In this connection it should also be mentioned that the Incorporated Law Society (the body which controls the Solicitors' profession) too, in the 'seventies, dramatically improved the professional education of its apprentices. It drew its aspiration from the Australian experience — not from the English model.

In the hurly-burly of events which occurred in the 'sixties and 'seventies two features of Irish law came prominently to the fore and have to be reckoned with immediately: the concept of Judicial Review and the Funamental Rights Provisions of the Constitution.

The Wexford Farmers Rates Case[3] can be used to illustrate these concepts. In this case the farmers contested that the rating system established by an 1852 Valuation Act infringed their rights under the constitution. The Supreme Court held that the State had indeed failed to respect the property rights of the citizen farmers concerned. The valuations had been fixed in 1854 and, in spite of the dramatic changes that had occurred in the meantime in agricultural production, and in spite of the emergence of serious inconsistencies and anomolies, had not been revised since then. The Court held that the Valuation Act was unconstitutional. From this we conclude, firstly that ordinary legislation must yield to the Constitution and, secondly, that the task of ensuring and supervising such compliance is entrusted to *the Courts*.

British Constitutional theory differs in that in their system *Parliament is supreme*. Whatever Parliament says *is* law, becomes law: there is no superior external criterion against which Parliament's actions can be easily measured. Furthermore, no supervisory role is given to the Courts in England in this respect.

The task given to the Courts in our Constitution therefore encourages greater *judicial activism*. The judges not only have a more prominent position in the system, they are also encouraged to participate in a more active way in the making of rules. Given their constitutional role, Irish judges are more likely to recognise that they have a role, especially in the elaboration and interpretation of the Constitution, which is not far short of judicial lawmaking.[4] This feature, of course, inevitably creates an occasional tension (not necessarily a bad thing) between the Courts on one hand and the Govenment and the Oireachtas on the other. When this feature coincided with the advent of what some people would term a *liberal jduciary* in a rapidly changing social scene (such as we had in the 'sixties and 'seventies) legal developments were bound to be exciting.

Fundamental Rights Provisions

The Wexford Farmers' case also highlights another feature of the Irish legal system. It shows, in contrast to the British system, that in Bunreacht na hÉireann we have, in Articles 40-44, a specified list of individual rights which are guaranteed and which cannot be taken away from the citizen by Government action or by legislation. The rights *expressly* protected in these articles include equality of treatment, personal liberty, freedom of expression, freedom of assembly, and the right to private property, among others. In the Wexford Farmers' Case the right to equal treatment and property rights were principally at issue.

In 1963, however, in *Ryan v. A.G.*,[5] in a landmark judgment, the Irish Courts recognised that there were *other* fundamental rights, not expressly referred to in the Constitution, which would also be protected by the Courts. In the case in question Mrs. Gladys Ryan contested the right of the Government to put flouride in the public water supply. She claimed that, although it was not expressly provided for in the Constitution, she had a '*right to bodily integrity*'. Although she lost her case on the facts, the Courts did hold in her favour on the legal point raised. There were indeed *other* unexpressed rights which the Courts would uphold. These rights, and I quote, 'are superior or antecedent to positive law' and cannot be taken away by ordinary, or man made laws passed by the State. Pandora's box was open. From this point onwards if the citizen could persuade the Court that a fundamental right existed he or she could resist Governmental encroachment on a constitutional basis. A flurry of activity ensued and since 1965 the Courts have recognised many additional rights as being fundamental to the citizen: the right to have recourse to the courts,[6] the right to marital privacy,[7] the right to travel,[8] the right to marry,[9] to mention but a few. And the catalogue of rights is not closed.

I repeat for emphasis that this was a judicial development, it was *the Courts* which recognised these rights as being fundamental and of Constitutional status. Moreover, in all these developments the Irish Courts became more outward looking: they drew their inspiration in this regard from International Conventions, from the decisions of the Supreme Court of the U.S.A., from Natural Law and from what one judge referred to as 'the dictates of justice'.

The significance of this development can hardly be exaggerated. Embracing the Natural Law philosophy, places enormous powers in the hands of the judiciary. In brief, it means that whenever the judges feel that a law is unjust, unfair or unreasonable they can refuse to follow it and can strike it down.[10]

One consequence of this it would seem is that when the judiciary gets used to handling somewhat vague concepts and principles such as reasonableness and justice it permeates their whole way of thinking, and it would appear that the Irish judge is much more willing to trade in the curency of broad principles than is his counterpart in England.[11] In England the judiciary has always shown a deep-seated distrust of stating rules in a general fashion.[12] It prefers to deal on an *as hoc* basis with each case as it arises: it also prefers to avoid generalisations.

What we have here then in Ireland today is a judiciary which is constitutionally conditioned to be *active* and cast in a role which makes it the *protector of individual liberty* against State excesses. In recent years we have been fortunate in having had, by and large, a *liberal*, courageous and increasingly self-reliant *judiciary* who recognise the indigenous qualities and the peculiar features of the Irish legal system. Occasionally, it is true that the Supreme Court may adopt a more conservative stand on particular issues. This is inevitable, and an understandable part of judicial law-making. Retrenchment will occur from time to time. In this context one thinks perhaps of the Norris case.[13] This should not, however, detract from the broad conclusion put forward here.[14] The judiciary has increased the status and power of the individual vis-a-vis the executive and legislative branches of Government, and it has provided the individual with a forum to which he may resort with confidence when he feels his rights are being infringed.

These developments have had interesting repercussions for the legal system generally.

It clearly indicates a move away from the Common law and from the English influence.

Instead of resorting to the traditional source for inspiration in the Constitutional area Irish lawyers have now begun to resort to the legal system of the United States of America. The parallels are closer and the precedents more relavent. The American Constitution had served as a model for the Irish Constitution. Like the Irish Constitution it is a written document, legislation is subject to judicial review, and the rights of the individual are well developed in the American jurisprudence. Furthermore, since its jurisprudence is in the English language it is readily accessible to Irish lawyers.

This outward looking approach was also aided, no doubt, by that other important development for the legal system which occurred during the period in question, namely, Ireland's accession to the European Economic Community. The effect of this in areas such as Commercial, Trade and Economic Law was enormous. Time does not permit us to explore this area, however, and the only reason I refer to it here is to support the observation that in the period under the examination the Irish legal system was being exposed to influences other than the traditional Common Law one coming from England. The legal systems which we came into contact with by joining the Common Market were systems which were of the Natural Law tradition, had written constitutions, and which showed familiarity with the cataloguing of fundamental rights and the concept of Judicial Review. Historical, cultural and religious affinities were rediscovered. Paradoxically, this exposure proved to our lawyers the correctness of moving away from the traditional monolithic influence and confirmed them in their self-reliance. We *were* different; other countries could express their uniqueness with distinctive individuality, and there was no reason why we too, as a legal system, could not move out from under the colonial shadow and go it alone.

Social and Political Environment

The rapidly changing social, economic and cultural changes in Ireland of the 'sixties provided the judiciary not only with the occasion but also with the opportunity of working out its new role as law makers and innovators. What has been called 'the decade of upheaval' — the 'sixties — was a period of changing values. It also witnessed emerging groupings and lobbies, groups who were willing to be more strident in the assertion of their rights. The changes continued at a faster rate in the 'seventies caused by accession to E.E.C., the oil crisis, the recession, etc. I will take two examples to illustrate some of the points I wish to make here. Firstly, I shall refer to the rise of feminism during the period and secondly, I shall examine the effect which the political instability in Northern Ireland has had for the legal system in the south.

The position of the woman in the legal system has improved in recent times. Some may suggest that it started from a low base. Be that as it may, in the last twenty five years, for example, the Courts in Ireland have recognised the constitutional right of a mother to the custody and care of her illegitimate child,[15] the right of women to serve on juries,[16] the right of the woman to independent tax assessment separate from her husband,[17] the right of access by married women to contraceptives (the right to marital privacy)[18] and the right to earn a livelihood without sexual discrimination.[19] Moreover, there has been progress too in the legislative sphere of which the family Home Protection Act 1976 and the Criminal Law (Rape) Act and the Family Law (Protection of Spouses and Children) Act, both passed in 1981, are but some examples.

From this it is clear that outstanding injustices in the legal system can be remedied if a persistent lobby takes up the cause. In the case of women's rights the international feminist movement found a response in Ireland and what one politician referred to as the 'well-heeled and articulate lobby' persisted in the political arena. Indeed some not so well-heeled ladies effectively took up the cudgels on behalf of battered wives and rape victims also. They were willing to sponsor litigation to bring their grievances before the Courts. This is important to remember in the context of judicial law reform. A court can only reform if given the opportunity to hear a case. It cannot take the initiative itself. Someone must bring the case before it. Although most prominent, women were not the only group to emerge in this regard. *Farmers*, as already noted, successfully financed a challenge on the Ratings Acts and *landlords* did the same in regard to the Rent Restrictions legislation.[20] The commitment of such lobbies enable the Courts to act; without such commitment from vigorous lobbies the courts might never be given an opportunity to consider the matter.

The Political Unrest in Northern Ireland

The second matter I would like to refer to in the present context is the political unrest in Northern Ireland. Since 1968 the political disturbances in the North have had a huge impact on life in the Republic. It is not surprising that the impact of these events would be significant in the legal system also. Apart from the positive reaction of the Government in dealing with security related matters since 1968 there has been a huge hidden transfer of resources and effort to areas which were related to the security of the State. The Government has had to deal with Constitutional Conferences (Sunningdale, the New Ireland Forum), cross-border security, the establishment and maintenance of Special Criminal Courts, political kidnappings, prolonged sieges, horsenappings, man hunts, hunger-strikes, jail riots, and extradition applications.

On analysis one can classify the reactions in the legal system to these activities under various headings.

(i)   I might first refer to Constitutional Reassessments
This involved not only the amendment of the Constitution in deference to Northern interests by deleting the fairly innocuous provision which recognised the special position of the Catholic Church, but also involved a more fundamental reassessment of the Constitution in the overall context of an all-Ireland solution. The New Ireland Forum exercise and the earlier Sunningdale discussions were examples of this. More recently, the Northern factor figured in the pro-life amendment debate, in the context of family planning legislation and is continuously raised in connection with the Constitutional ban on divorce.

(ii)   Next, I must mention the Emergency Legislation
Under this heading we can refer to the legislation which was passed by successive governments to deal with what were called political and terrorist type crimes. The establishment of the Special Criminal Court, the constitutional declaration of a state of emergency and the new Offences Against the State Act, and various Criminal Justice Acts passed in the 'seventies and most recently amended in 1984 can be cited. All of these were measures designed to strengthen the powers of the State in dealing with what were seen to be abnormal criminal activities which could not be handled by the ordinary criminal process. The legislation — by and large applicable to scheduled offences only — saw the establishment of the Special Criminal Court which dispenses with the necessity of a jury trial, the relaxation of the ordinary rules of evidence, the extention of garda powers of questioning, arrest and detention, the creation of new offences, the extention of jurisdiction to crimes committed in Northern Ireland, and, lastly the increase of penalties for certain offences. In so far as the legislation represented a departure from the minimum accepted standards it was criticised by liberal groups as being as unwarranted threat to individual liberties.

Not surprisingly some of this legislation found its way into the Courts. The Criminal Law (Jurisdiction) Bill was referred to the Supreme Court by President Ó Dálaigh[21] and gave us 'the thundering disgrace' episode which ended in the President's resignation. Kevin Boland went to the Courts[22] claiming that the Irish Government had acted *ultra vires* in signing the Sunningdale Agreement and several individuals prosecuted under this legislation, claimed in various ways that their personal rights had been infringed. Ironically, the exercise of these powers resulted in more cases coming before the Courts and gave the Courts more opportunities to clarify and define the personal rights of the individual under the constitution. The Courts were given the opportunity to clarify some personal rights which they might not have had if this legislation had not been introduced. One had the scene of so-called 'repressive legislation' being introduced by the Government; liberal and civil liberty groups opposing it; individuals contesting it before the Courts and the Courts then being provided with the opportunity of giving a better definition of the individual's rights.

One of the consequences of all this is that now we have, in this State existing side by side with each other, not one, but *two* systems of criminal justice. For political/terrorist types of crime we have special offences, special and extended police powers, more relaxed forms of evidence, special non-jury courts, different penalties and segregated detention.

In this duality of approach personnel involved in the administration of justice must be doubly careful if their actions are not to be misinterpreted. The Gardaí and the judiciary in particular must be sensitive to public perceptions. Public confidence in the institutions of the State is not promoted by the emergence of the so-called Heavy Gang or by other police excesses or indeed by the indecent haste of the judiciary in the McGlinchy extradition proceedings. Public support for our legal system is not elicited by the sight of our judiciary assembling hastily at night on St. Patrick's weekend in the unheated atmosphere of the Four Courts to dispatch to another jurisdiction a man who could certainly have been charged with serious crimes in this jurisdiction. I have always felt that justice moved with measured steps and at a deliberate pace. The element of haste, displayed in the McGlinchy proceedings somewhat offends my concept of fair play.

And it is not only the judiciary and the Gardaí who are in danger of losing face with the public. In recent years we have seen the offices of the Minister for Justice, the Minister for Defence, the Attorney General and the Director of Public Prosecutions all come under fire.

Indeed, the office of the President himself during the Ó Dálaigh/Donnegan affair, did not escape. The Kerry Babies Tribunal is the most recent, and perhaps, the most spectacular target for public criticism. It seems to be open season for the institutions associated with law, order and justice. And this is worrying. Why, we may ask, is the public losing confidence?

No one can deny that very serious problems have been presented to the Government by the political disturbances which have plagued this island since 1968. And I would like to emphasise that I am in no way condoning many of the senseless atrocities that have been committed in the name of various political philosophies since the recent troubles began. But there is another danger and that is the danger that genuine and sincere critics of Governmental actions are silenced in this atmosphere for fear of being tar-daubed as 'fellow-travellers'. A very subtle censorship exists: to express an adverse opinion of the actions of the institutions of the State in the present circumstance one runs the risk of being branded as supporting illegal activities. This, fact too, must be recognised.

I grew up with a very familiar appreciation of the Gardaí as part of the local community, whose crime detection rate was high partly, no doubt, because serious crimes were not so numerous as they are nowadays, but also I suggest because the Gardaí were, and still are in many parts of the country, very much integrated into the Community. They were trusted by their Community; they had easy and natural access to community information and suspects were frequently much more visible to them in the environment of twenty years ago.

I very much fear nowadays, however, that pressures of one sort or another are forcing Gardaí into a role which is very different from their traditional role. Extended powers designed to combat political subversives are regularly used against non-political offenders. It was stated in the Dáil last year[23] that in the previous 12 months over 2,000 arrests had been made under Section 30 of the Offences Against the State Act and that only 1 in 9 had been prosecuted. The Section is being used for ordinary criminal offences for which it was never designed. Shades of the Prevention of Terrorism Act in the United Kingdom!! It is only natural that Gardaí who are given extended powers will use these powers whenever and wherever they can. The pressures on them to get results are great. If through nods and winks they are encouraged in this by the politicians, so much the easier for them. And one can only sympathise with them in many cases because with the rising crime rate their task is becoming very difficult and much more hazardous. What is happening in all of this, of course, is that the gardaí, because of this seepage from the regime established for subversives, are getting a different perspective of their own role. Instead of seeing their job as one of collecting evidence, making an arrest and proferring a charge, the gardaí now increasingly see their job as one of securing a confession. And this could be dangerous. As well as putting individual rights at risk, it minimises judicial functions, brings the law into disrepute and alienates the public. This fear I think is what was at the bottom of the recent debate on the Criminal Justice Bill. I think we must be very careful that in seeking to combat political subversives we do not tear to shreds the very fabric of our legal system. Unless our reactions are prudent and cautious our last state will be worse than our first.

The real danger of all this is obvious: persons operating the system soon come to imagine that the special powers given for the special offences are the norm, and that the ordinary rules of criminal law and procedure no longer apply even for 'ordinary' criminal offences. Normal standards relevant to normal conditions in a civilised state become eroded; an inevitable seepage occurs and what appears necessary to cope with political offences tends to become engrained in the system for 'ordinary' criminal activities. In this scenario temporary tends to become permanent; the specific measure tends to become general; the exceptional provision tends to become the rule. Measures tolerated for exceptional threats become recommended practices for less menancing social deviations. One must acknowledge that there may in the circumstances, be great personal stress on individual Gardaí throughout the country and we must not be lured into thinking that because they all wear similar uniforms, all Gardaí think the same way. It must be well nigh impossible, however, for dissenting Gardaí to voice their views without putting their careers in jeopardy in the present atmosphere.

Conclusion

One cannot hope to summarise comprehensively, but I might end where I began: with Mrs. Josie Airey. An oppressed individual; a woman; alone and without the support of an identifiable lobby — before the value of group action was recognised; with little advice except from accidental sources — a student advice centre and a brother in America; convinced of her rights; willing to take on the State in an international forum and eventually succeeding in having her position vindicated. Individual rights and external influences are evident. Add to this a frequently active judiciary (liberal more often than not) willing to support the individual from unjustifiable State encroachments and one has a picture of the most salient features of today's legal system. All in all, while we must be constantly vigilant, the outside influences are increasingly encouraging us to be self-reliant. The combination of these outside influences and our own increasing self-confidence indicate that we have much to be proud of in our legal system. And while dangers to the system abound because of the political disturbances, as long as we recognise these threats and appreciate the risks, there is no reason to believe that we cannot preserve untarnished our own identity in our own legal system.

Justice is portrayed as a blind goddess holding aloft the scales of righteousness. As a people it will take all our collective and individual wisdom, our courage and our dedication to hold these scales in equilibrium.

NOTES

1.   1979 2 HRR 305.
2.   See footnote 10 and 11 *infra*.
3.   *Brennan v. A.G.*, 1983, ILRM 449.
4.   'While these rights are expressly given by the Constitution, they are not the only constitutional rights. The High Court and Supreme Court have held that the Constitution indicates that there are other rights protected by it and that their formulation is a matter for the judges of the High Court and, on appeal, for those of the Supreme Court. They thus have the power to recognise and enforce constitutional rights which are not expressly stated in the Constitution. To most people this would seem to be a function of the legislature only, and in many ways, this exciting feature is the most unusual aspect of the Constitution. Judges have become legislatures and have the advantage that they do not have to face an opposition.' Kenny J., The Advantages of a Written Constitution Incorporating a Bill of Rights. 30 N.I.L.Q. 189, at 196-6.
5.   1965, I.R. 294.
6.   *Macauley v. Minister for Posts and Telegraphs*, 1966, I.R. 345.
7.   *McGee v. Attorney General*, 1974, I.R. 284.
8.   *The State (M) v. Attorney General*, 1979, I.R. 73.
9.   Kelly, The Irish Constitution (2nd ed.) 486.

10. See Carroll J., in *Morgan v. Park Developments*. 1983, I.L.M.R. 156, at 160. 'It seems to me that no law which could be described as 'harsh and absurd' or which the courts could say was unreasonable and unjustifiable in principle (as did the English Courts) could also be constitutional'.

11. Apart from Carroll J., cited in previous note see also Walsh J., in *Purtill v. Athlone U.D.C.*, 1968, I.R. 205. Contrast also as an example of judicial courage the Irish Supreme court in *McNamara v. E.S.B.*, 1975, I.R. 1 with the House of Lords in *British Railway Board v. Harrington*, 1972, A.C. 877.

12. See Dias and Markesinis, Tort Law.

13. *Norris v. Attorney General*, Sup. Ct., 22 April 1983 (Unreptd. as yet).

14. None of these rights are unlimited. The restrictions that exist, however, in the Constitution itself 'are aimed not at limiting, but at enriching, the flourishing and enjoyment of fundamental rights'. See Redmond, Fundamental Rights in Irish Constitutional Law, in Morality and the Law. Ed. D.M. Clarke, p. 97.

15. *G. V. An Bord Uchtala*, 1980, I.R. pg. 32.

16. *deBurca v. A.G.*, 1976, I.R. 38.

17. *Murphy v. A.G.*, 1982, I.R. 241.

18. *McGee v. Attorney General*, 1974, I.R. 284.

19. *Murtagh Properties v. Cleary*, 1972, I.R. 330.

20. *Blake v. A.G.*, 1982, I.R. 117.

21. In re Art. 26 and the Criminal Law (Jurisdiction) Bill, 1975. 1977, I.R. 129.

22. *Boland v. An Taoiseach*, 1974, I.R. 338.

23. 'Figures issued by the Department of Justice show that more than 2,000 people have been arrested under section 30 of [the Offences Against the State] Act in the past year. In 1972 the figure in this respect was 200, so the increase since then has been dramatic. However, the ratio of people charged as a result of these arrests is one in nine. That would not seem to indicate that there is any value in the arrest and detention provision being proposed in the present Bill. Rather, it indicates that there is a tendency to use section 30 in what can be termed only a very loose manner'. Mr. P. De Rossa, T.D., Dáil Debates, 19 January 1984, col. 365.

Expanding an Island Ethic

My story begins on the South Side of Chicago where I grew up with one certain conviction: I was Irish. A third generation Irish father never told me there was any difference between 'American' Irish and 'native' Irish. As far as he was concerned, we were a thoroughbred transplant from Inishderg and it was only by an accident of opportunity that we were living in Chicago. My illusions began young with the nuns helping to foster these illusions by putting me in a shamrock-studded chorus line singing Cockles and Mussells. Guaranteed Irish! Later, I was to marry a native Irishman who cleared up my illusion once and for all. I was American, not Irish. So be it. I am in Ireland now for over ten years and my contrasting feelings about Ireland are similar to Albert Camus', the French writer, who speaks of New York City as a love who annoys you, overwhelms you and evokes tears of emotion and all-consuming fury![1]   It is not easy to be indifferent to Ireland.

My topic, 'Expanding an Island Ethic' looks at ethics or morality as it has been most pervasively understood in Ireland at least during the last century.[2] But, first, what is ethics? Ethics refers to our beliefs about what comprises a happy life, what makes for a worthwhile society; ethics also includes our beliefs about what behaviour *contributes to or frustrates* the achievement of a worthwhile society. Finally, ethics wonders about what features of character are worth cultivating. These aspects are all interconnected in most ethical systems. Beliefs about what is 'right' and 'wrong' and what kind of people we should become — these only make sense when closely linked to our beliefs about what comprises a 'worthwhile' sociey. Inevitably, controversies arise in ethics over deciding what is a worthwhile or valuble society and *how human beings can best achieve it*.[3]

Ethics is not just a set of beliefs, however. It also includes reasons for accepting some values rather than others — the assumption being that if no reasons can be given in support of moral values, then they are no better than arbitrary whim or purely emotional reactions to life's situations. But what is the Irish 'sense' of ethics which has dominated most of the last century?

Content of 'traditional ethic'

One prevailing understanding of morality has been reinforced by families, the vast majority of schools, the pulpit and even the Government.[4] The content of this Irish ethic, largely determined by a 95% Catholic population, has been a litany of forbidden behaviour based on the Ten Commandments, laced with a generous dollup of puritanism: lying, cheating, stealing were clearly forbidden. But the sixth and ninth Commandments became a fixation of one's formative years. James Joyce describes the obsession with carnal sin that torments Stephen Daedalus in *Portrait of the Artist.* Joyce writes: 'His body to which he had yielded was dying . . . Into the grave with it! Nail it down into a wooden box, the corpse . . . Thrust it out of men's sight into a long hole in the ground, into the grave, to rot, to feed the mass of its creeping worms and to be devoured by scuttling plump-bellied rats.'[5]

Fornication and impure thoughts, and how not to enjoy them obsessed the moral imagination of many an Irish mind and not only in the pages of literature. Morality narrowly focussed on contraception, divorce, abortion, homosexuality and sterilisation. There was no a la carte. It was all or nothing. An impartial psychologist coming to Ireland might well wonder at a celibate clergy exercising so much energy concentrating on the sexual behaviour of other people!

Some Irish scholars claim that this preoccupation with sex is really a distortion of the true Irish character — a distortion of an otherwise non-puritan tradition. This view goes on to claim that it was Queen Victoria, with her country's prudish ways, which were transported across the Irish Sea only to harass this country ever since.[6] But this view offers much too simplistic an explanation. A preoccupation with sex in morality is a universal feature of the Roman Catholic Church. For example, just several months ago, Pope John Paul II concluded a series of ten lectures, which he called a 'personal campaign' aimed at reinforcing the Catholic Church's complete ban on artificial birth control, abortion, sterilisation and test tube fertilisation.[7]

However, it is possible, by simply reading the works of the early Church fathers, to *understand if not appreciate* this fixation on matters sexual. Along with documents on the superior value of virginity, Father such as Jerome, Augustine and Tertullian regarded the sexual act, even in marriage, with a constantly anxious eye and exhibit an inordinate compulsion to persuade couples to abstain as much as possible. [8]

The Irish scholars' theory of Queen Victoria's role in this distorted focus of ethics is not only historically short-sighted, but it also does not make clear what is achieved by *continuing* to attribute today's deficiencies to an English Queen long since deceased! Be that as it may, the net effect of this narrow focus in morality was that ethics became isolated from most areas of Irish public life: business, farming, politics, journalism, legal affairs, health-care, education: *all insulated from moral scrutiny and relieved of the burdens of social accountability.* [9]

Catholic morality as taught in Ireland also came packaged with a special set of other beliefs that were meant to rationally explain why the moral rules taught were the *only true ones* available. This set of beliefs consisted of the following: God as the Creator of all nature has given human beings the gift of reason; by means of this reason, human beings can find, *in nature*, the rules for moral behaviour and civil law. These beliefs are usually referred to as a Theory of Natural Law. [10] However, the process of discovering our moral obligations through nature only *seemed* very straightforward.

St. Thomas Aquinas, a thirteenth century defender of Natural Law theory, indicates otherwise. He makes clear that *not everybody* can draw *correct* moral insights from nature. Aquinas claims: 'Whatever arguments are brought forward against the doctrines of faith are conclusions incorrectly derived from the first and self-evident principles imbedded in nature.' [11] In other words, to derive *correct* moral truths from nature, one must use reason *properly*. But using reason *properly* means that one must reach the same conclusions as the hierarchical Catholic Church. Somehow one gets the clear impression that there is a theological sleight of hand here and the cards are stacked against any who would disagree!

However, if rules for behaviour are so obviously available from nature, how can we explain the *fact of moral disagreement*? Is it necessary to conclude that any views which do not agree with Church teachings are a result of faulty reason, or as Aquinas elsewhere says, a result of sin or passion?[12] This conclusion, based on a stance of moral imperialism, would seem clearly unacceptable.

I would suggest that moral disagreement exists because nature's processes are not subject to just one interpretation. In fact, a stronger claim is called for: *no moral interpretation can be derived directly from nature at all.* Let me illustrate: ten thousand people could agree on all of the details of the physiological processes of human reproduction and no amount of pondering over these facts will make it obvious or self-evident that artificial contraception is immoral.[13] In order to arrive at this conclusion, one has to accept *on faith* that God has made nature and human beings in such a way that humans are forbidden to exercise discretion in altering the processes of nature.[14]

Church teachings on natural law are couched in terms of humans not 'tampering with' or 'interfering in' nature. The language itself has emotive overtones which seem to suggest that the moral issues in question have been decided in advance by the very terms used in stating the problem. To many, perhaps, this warning about altering processes of nature is puzzling. It seems apparent that humans do regularly alter, redirect or interrupt natural processes and we consider our interventions as morally justified. Examples abound in the practice of medicine: artificial limbs, hormone injections, kidney transplants, artificial insemination by husband, cardiac pace makers, even the casual vitamin supplements are human efforts at modifying or improving on existing natural processes.

What is so frequently presented in the Church's defence, as a purely *reasoned* position is, on inspection, *a set of theological beliefs* about which interventions are moral and which immoral. These collateral theological beliefs require people to accept the Catholic Church claim that it is the only true interpreter of morality.[15] It becomes then a question of wondering how some persons or institutions become moral authorities?

Moral Authority

Authority is usually understood as a form of power or right to require certain behaviour of others, to enforce orders or laws, or to take certain actions and decisions for other people.[16] Furthermore, one becomes an authority in different ways: some, like religious institutions, claim to have Divinely conferred authority; others are authorised by national election or by official appointment. Finally, one can become an authority, without official designation, simply by showing special expertise or example in a certain area of competence. For example, Ireland laments the few remaining authorities on thatching roofs.

If an authority is to be considered *credible and effective* in its own special area, it is expected to give evidence of competence. Competence is generally shown by *expertise* and *example*. A credible authority will not only have knowledge about the area of alleged competence, but, given the opportunity, would be able to demonstrate and even excell in the skills which define the area of claimed expertise. Many who live in Cork city, for example, believe that Jack Lynch was the authority, *par excellence* on politics. For this reason, no matter who the encumbent Government is, Jack Lynch is said to nevertheless be *the real Taoiseach*!

Now, given this normal expectation that an authority *show* expertise and example, how do *moral authorities* fare in Ireland? But first, what is a moral authority? A moral authority is usually understood as an expert in doing a number of things: *identifying values* in a given culture which are essential in human living; being able to *explain* why these values are so significant and *providing reasons* why certain ways of behaving are preferable to others if a certain type of worthwhile society is to be achieved.[17]

The dominant moral authority in Ireland over the last century has been the Roman Catholic Church. This Church claims to be the teacher of truth, Divinely authorised, and guaranteed certain in its moral and dogmatic teachings. However, claiming Divine authority always raises the obstinate question: How can fallible human beings be so confident about knowing God's mind?[18] The lines of communication between the Church and God must be far superior to those provided by Telecom Eireann! But if the Church is to be a *credible* authority, Irish people might expect representatives of the Institution, including political proponents of Church positions, to demonstrate their expertise and example in morality.[19] The scene of chauffeur-driven Mercedes cars by political officials would not seem to be a convincing illustration of *moral example* in a country where large numbers of unemployed have barely enough to survive.

Liam O'Flaherty enjoys expatiating on the alleged expertise and example of Church officials in the area of education: The parish priest, O'Flaherty writes, 'is most commonly seen making a cautious approach to the Education Office, where he has all sorts of complaints to lodge and all sorts of suggestions to make. Every book recommended by the education authorities for the schools is examined by him, and if he finds a single idea in any of them that might be likely to inspire thought of passion, then he is up in arms at once. Like an army of black beetles on the march, he and his countless brothers invade Dublin and lay siege to the official responsible . . . Woe to them . . . all the ministers and responsible officials.' [20]

The humour of O'Flaherty aside, Church authorities in Ireland have abundant opportunity to show their expertise in morality. For example, they might, by participating in forums of public discussion, make clear the reasons behind Church moral teachings — whether on contraception, abortion or divorce, reasons which might make plausible the claim that Roman Catholic moral views be enshrined in the Constitution and, furthermore, be the basis for future legislative changes. [21]   The argument is often heard that such views are in the *majority* in the Republic and, therefore, should be entitled to be the basis for civil or criminal law. [22] But this argument might not convince increasing numbers of so-called 'minority members' in the Republic. Furthermore, is the Catholic Church willing to be *consistent* and ask Catholics in Poland, Russia, or even Northern Ireland, to bow to the 'majority' ideologies obtaining in those countries? The sheer logic of the *majority argument* would seem to require this.

If the Chruch and its proponents are, however, able but unwilling to show their expertise in the area of morality, the question arises — *why*? Several possibilities might be suggested: Are ordinary people of Ireland considered to be incapable of understanding the reasons for their moral beliefs? Are the laity not trusted to choose immortal ends before mortal if they see they have choices? Or, do Church authorities fear that if they try to explain, the attempt will be unconvincing? Are Church moral authorities, themselves, unpersuaded by the very beliefs they promote as certain? Finally, is it perhaps the case that Churchmen have not been trained to see that there is a need to explain moral beliefs so they are able to win a level of mature and responsible commitment? [23] It is not obvious which of these diagnoses approaches the correct one.

While the Church maintains a reticence to publicly explain and yet a readiness to exhort obedience, questions are surfacing in Ireland which seem to be probing for the missing explanations — questions which have perhaps been long felt but were buried in resignation. For example, one wonders how many families continued to have more children when the number they had deeply strained their psychological, economic and spiritual resources — continuing to procreate because they were taught contraception was wrong? [24] One puzzles how many women felt especially alienated by an all-male celibate clergy who, without obvious expertise, have so shaped the traditional model of the *moral Irish woman*. [25] One contemporary woman author speaks of the model in these terms: 'Man's vision of woman is not objective but an uneasy combination of what *he wishes her to be* and *what he fears her to be*, and it is to this mirror image that woman has had to comply.' [26]

From the collective unconscious of the Irish people, was there any wondering what ethics had to say about the despair of impoverished lives, [27] about staggering levels of unemployment, political phone-tapping and gross inequities in taxation, about apparent exploitation of Irish labour and natural resources by some multinationals. How many failed to understand why there was no legal provision for divorce where two people were psychologically destroying each other and yet the couple down the road just got a Church annulment? [28] How many non-Catholics could not understand talk of ecumenism and *inter-faith respect* while priests continued to require that any children of a 'mixed-marriage' be raised in the Catholic faith? [29]

If the questions were there, they were rarely articulated and this repression of inquiry would have ramifications throughout Irish life. [30] In effect, moral reflection and examination of values were considered dangerous since one could never predict the outcome. One wonders what Socrates would think — the great Greek philospher who taught that 'the unexamined life is not worth living!' But if questioning is dismissed in an area of such presumed importance, a more pervasive reticence to questioning the *status quo* develops. Ireland, over the last one-hundred years, reinforced a national morality which is largely monolithic and has remained so by being carefully insulated from alien challenges.

Protectionism

A uniform morality is relatively easy to preserve on a small island in the middle of the Atlantic Ocean, especially if protectionist measures are used which meet with little opposition from successive Governments. The Censorship Board, in existence since 1930, protected this island's enclosed morality not only from pornography (such as it was), but from the literary genius of contemporary authors and those long since dead:[31] Sean O'Faolain estimates that, between 1929 and 1955, a greater proportion of native writers of note were banned in Ireland than in Russia.[32] Perhaps it occurred to many that this kind of protectionism is more appropriate in a parent-child relationship than for fostering mature and responsible moral persons.[33]

Meanwhile, this island isolation is still viewed by some as a positive advantage for preserving Ireland's moral reputation intact. I wonder, though, can this isolationist stance be sustained? And, even if it is possible, is it desirable?

A highly protected morality tends to become a highly defensive morality. Defensiveness surfaced in generous doses on all sides in the long debates of the recent abortion referendum, an event that perhaps many would prefer to forget — like a bad dream. The referendum was widely criticised for *introducing divisiveness* into the country but this claim has not been given with convincing argument. It seems, rather, that there is a kind of denial at work here and, simultaneously, an irrepressible urge to keep the surface waters tranquil. Disagreement existed prior to public debate. The people in Ireland may not have realised the extent of mnoral disagreement and the referendum became the *occasion* to voice differing views. What was only a forum for discussing the disagreements could not be blamed for creating these differences.

The abortion referendum was anything but a single issue challenging the moral monolith. There were many complex issues intertwined: legislating for morality, the non-availability of contraceptives for the unmarried, women's rights in child-bearing, conditions that might justify abortion, ostracising of unwed mothers and, finally, apparent neglect of the children already on this island. Perhaps the Irish people also felt *painfully unequipped with the necessary skills for dialoging for understanding and constructive resolution rather than scoring points!*[34]

The moral example of some Church officials suffered a blow with many according to social commentators in the wake of the referendum. Sincerely religious people were outraged at the overt paternalism of some priests and bishops in the pulpits admonishing the faithful to either vote 'yes' at the polling booth or feel the guilt of murder on their souls. It may be that many Irish people felt disappointed that the traditional moral authorities were apparently aggravating the divisions and intensifying the emotional barriers to dialogue. Many would subsequently argue that the intimidating tactics reduced credibility in Church claims about freedom of conscience. Perhaps today there is a qualified hope that more constructive discussion and less denigration will characterise any future referendum on divorce.

In the end, it may remain for the Irish social historian of tomorrow to show that, while Church and State fully intended protectionist measures to safeguard the strength of moral uniformity, the position had quite the opposite effect. The social historian may have the evidence to show that a moral system can be sheltered from the challenges of disagreement but it will be seen, correspondingly, to be insecure. On the other hand, the evidence of history may show that an Irish ethic which meets the challenge of dialoging with differing views may be praised and strengthened, and even emulated, by being confident in itself.[35]

Expanding the traditional ethic?

So a final question needs to be asked: How has this island ethic of the last century affected Irish society? Is the Republic of Ireland in 1985 very different from other western societies or does it rather experience many of the same moral dilemmas which are found in other European countries?

Last year at least 4,500 women went to England to have an abortion.[36] On the family front, the statistics on broken marriages are still only the tip of the iceberg according to official estimates.[37] It has also been estimated that, every year, up to sixty people commit the crime of bigamy in Ireland and the State and the Catholic Church, with their contradictory laws on marriage, help to condone and conceal the fact.[38] One can hardly blame the couples involved. Where law reform fails to keep pace with reality, the end result is bound to be forced hypocrisy. Population expansion continues to strain the resources of a limited economy and yet is combined with an insistent demand that the Irish State provide jobs for an exploding population.[39] It seems not to occur to the politicians or Churchmen (idly wrangling over the availability of contraceptives!) that Ireland might consider *restraining population growth* if moral responsibility to future generations is to be more than a pious platitude.

It is hardly necessary to expand the list of ways in which contemporary Ireland shares the same moral dilemmas with other European countries. In attacks on the elderly, in the incidence of drug or alcohol abuse, and the increase in city crime, Ireland may be a few years behind other countries, but it is clearly following the same path. Given these social facts, some might, nevertheless, object and claim that Ireland has the problems I've mentioned *precisely because* this island has *rejected* its traditional ethic. However, I would like to suggest a different interpretation of Irish experience during the last century. *It is because the dominant view of morality in Ireland failed to relate to lived experience* that it provided little guidance in the complexity of modern living.[40] And this brings me back to my basic contention: that a theological ethic of absolute commands, which is predominantly about sex, based on a theory of nature that cannot be defended, is irrelevant to the needs of twentieth century living!

In general, Irish people have not been accustomed to think they have a choice about their morality: either its content, its authority or its application. The pervasive assumption has long been that morality is a *completed system of divinely authorised and certain beliefs.*[41] To modify this way of thinking about morality may seem, to many, like a sacrifice of the *security* that certainty brings.[42] While appreciating this concern, I am, nevertheless, reminded of the American philospher and educationalist, John Dewey, who claimed that a quest for certainty down through the ages has held human societies captive and made morality into a static enterprise. A quest for certainty, Dewey continues, prevented many human communities from taking the daring and innovative steps required to provide a morality that makes a social difference — a morality which could genuinely affect the *quality of human living.*[43] With this in mind, it may be worth wondering whether the Irish traditional ethic could be expanded so that narrowness of scope and defensiveness of authority would not define this island's morality to the world outside?

But what is an 'expanded' island ethic and what would it have to offer as an improvement on the traditional ethic of the last one hundred years? Briefly, (1) expansion would encourage a changed understanding of the *scope* of ethics to include areas of decision-making which have the power to radically determine or frustrate the achievement of a happy and worthwhile human society. Wherever decisions are being made, not just by us as individuals, but *for us* by Government, Church, legal and economic authorities — these decisions have value assumptions and moral implications. These areas of decision-making are *moral* precisely and to the extent that they affect the well-being of human lives.[44]

A school system which recognises the validity of an expanded ethic might introduce programmes encouraging skills of moral reasoning for reflection in a wide range of applied ethics: legal, corporation, medical, environment, industrial relations, economic ethics — all providing potential material for moral intelligence and imagination.[45] Students of such a school would take it for granted that there must be viable structures for *accountability* in every level of Irish society because these students will have been taught that moral responsibility requires accountability.[46] Furthermore, these students would not accept 'appeals to authority' as an answer to a query unless the authority in question had proved itself credible on the criteria discussed earlier. (2) An expanded ethic would also have to be prepared to argue for broadening the base of respected decision-makers and moral authorities — for expanding the very concept of 'moral authority'. A morality, monopolised by one Church and a coterie of political apologists for that Church, might be enlarged to encourage a sharing of grassroots insight, intelligence and social vision.[47] An expanded ethic would not be incompatible with religion unless a particular form of religion insisted that its spokespersons were the only moral authorities to be heard. (3) Garrett Fitzgerald attempted something of an expanded ethic in his highly controversial Constitutional Crusade — a courageous proposal, many thought, but then one wonders why it is, nevertheless, accumulating Dail dust and little debate. Was the rhetoric of a 'crusade' perhaps ill-chosen and off-putting for a nation of people still hurting from the hatred exhibited in Irish religious history? An expanded ethic might just signal to the Northern population that gestures towards unity are not intended to be merely charades of political opportunism.

Admittedly, an expanded island ethic would mean a sacrifice of the security promised by certainty. But the traditional ethic has yet *to show that its promise of certainty is not an illusion*. The promise of certainty which offers such comfort may, in the end, be more of a consoling refuge than a constructive resource! An expanded ethic is one alternative to Ireland's traditional ethic — an alternative which does not necessarily require a rejection of Ireland's dominant religion. Modifications in the authoritative stance of this religion would, however, be a requirement for compatibility with an 'expanded ethic'. An expanded island ethic being proposed does not assume tht morality is completed or unchanging or certain. Furthermore, an expanded ethic could never be *imposed* on Irish people — for that would run contrary to the basic assumption of such an ethic: the assumption that human beings *cannot be commanded to be moral!*

In the end, it is a choice for Irish people to make — a choice of what kind of society Ireland will become in this next century. A contemporary psychologist offers as a final note what may be a welcome reassurance: 'Only a ghost wallows around in his past, explaining himself with self-descriptors based on a life lived through. You are what you choose today,' and need not be confined to the choices of a congealed past — a past which looks especially glorious to those who never had to live in it.[48]

NOTES

1. Albert Camus, *Lyrical and Critical Essays,* New York, Alfred A. Knopf, 1968, p. 185.
2. Two surveys published during 1984 are renewed efforts to get systematic information on the moral/religious beliefs in Ireland. See: 'A Survey of Senior Students' Attitudes towards religion, morality, education, 1982' Part I in *Religious Life Review,* Nov.-Dec., 1984, 325-331 and Part II in same journal, Jan.-Feb., 1985, 39-49. Cf. *Irish Values and Attitudes,* The Irish Report of the European Values Systems Study, (Dublin: Dominican Publications, 1984). A recently published study which would seem to corroborate the view stated here is: *Is Irish Catholicism Dying?,* Peadar Kirby (Dublin and Cork: Mercier Press, 1984). I would agreee with Kirby that efforts at 'updating' have been made in the Catholic Church in Ireland especially since Vatican II. Trocaire deserves special mention in Kirby's book though he admits that 'equivalent groups set up to tackle injustice *at home* cannot be said to have shown the same vigour.' (p. 26) The rather narrow focus on sex is reiterated by Kirby when he places the analysis at the grass-roots level: 'Ask any average young Irish person as to what moral issue worries the Catholic bishops and they will *not* reply social injustice or nuclear war but rather sexual immorality.' (p. 28) Cf. 'Legalism and Irish Catholicism' by Tom Inglis in *Social Studies* Vol. 7. No. 1. Winter 1982-83, 33-41. Numerous articles in Irish journals such as *Furrow, Doctrine and Life, Religious life Review, Social Studies,* and *Irish Theological Studies* are encouraging as signs of vitality in Irish reflection. While a variety of points of view are expressed there on a wide range of issues, these variant views are seldom expressed in public forums more readily accessible to the vast majority of Irish

people. As a result, the dominant perception as stated in my paper does not change significantly if at all. By and large, the pulpit and schools shape the perceptions.

3. A number of fine books are given to this understanding of ethics but the following studies and collections of essays are especially helpful: R.S. Peters, *Ethics and Education*, London, George Allen and Unwin Ltd., 1970; Mary Warnock, *Ethics Since 1900*, 2nd ed., London, Oxford University Press, 1968; Milton Fisk, *Ethics and Society*, Sussex, England, Harvester Press Ltd., 1980; Stephen Toulmin, *Reason in Ethics*, London, Cambridge Univ. Press, 1964; Arthur Caplan and Daniel Callahan, *Ethics in Hard Times*, (eds.), New York, Plenum Press, 1981); Daniel Callahan and H. Tristam Engelhardt, Jr. *The Roots of Ethics,* New York, Plenum Press, 1981.

4. In saying this is the 'prevailing' understanding of morality or ethics, I am allowing for individuals (both clerical, religious and lay) whose attitudes and involvement in social projects would provide counter-examples for the claims I make here.

5. James Joyce, *A Portrait of the Artist as a Young Man*, New York, The Viking Press, 1964, p. 112.

6. See 'Stability and Ambivalence' by Professor Seán Ó Tuama, printed in this volume. Cf. Patrick C. Power, *Sex and Marriage in Ancient Ireland*, Dublin and Cork, Mercier Press, 1976.

7. *Irish Times,* 29 November 1984. It is the language of Pope John Paul II which reflects a philosophy of marital sexuality that may increasingly alienate contemporary married persons. The Pope claims that married couples who learn to resist the 'lust of the flesh' and practice sexual continence will enrich their relationship. There is a danger (in terms of loss of credibility) that John Paul II will be seen to take a retrograde step here by simplistically identifying sexual expression of love with 'lust'.

8. It is ironic that Sts. Jerome and Augustine should write so vehemently of woman as temptress and sexuality as clearly an inferior state to celibacy when their own early days were incontinent. Much of St. Jerome's thought on these subjects can be found in his epistles and, for Augustine and Tertullian, throughout many of their central works. An excellent and scholarly volume of essays which studies images of women in the Jewish and Christian traditions is Rosemary Radford Reuther (ed.), *Religion and Sexism*, New York, Simon and Schuster, 1974.

9. The broadening of focus and concern in moral understanding will not change significantly in Ireland until changes occur in the ethos and curricula of primary and secondary schools, until education of primary teachers is broadened to include a vision of morality as a human enterprise to improve the quality of life at all levels in society. Last but clearly not least, a dominant force for change toward social accountability would be a radical change in the educational process of diocesan priests in Ireland. The pulpit is still the main image-communicator of the Church in Ireland and homilies from the pulpit are not generally seen to 'stretch the categories' of lay persons' understanding of morality. See: Padraig Hogan, 'The Question of Ethos in Schools', *Furrow*, vol. 35, No. 11, Nov. 1984, 693-703; Donal Murray, 'Values for a New Continent', *Furrow*, Vol. 35, No. 4, April 1984, 211-224. Donal Murray, as Titular

Bishop of Glendalough and Auxiliary to the Archbishop of Dublin is also concerned with narrowness of moral focus. He writes: 'It must not, therefore, be allowed to seem that our sphere of interests as Christians is narrow, that we are concerned predominantly with *sexual* morality, or with *religious* freedom, or with internal Church affairs. The sphere of interest for those who wish to be faithful to the Christian heritage is nothing less than the whole of human life' (p. 225). Finally, Donal Dorr challenges the prevailing understanding of institutionalized Christian morality in his article, 'The Challenge of Technology' in *Social Studies* Vol. 3, No. 1,Feb. 1974, 51-58.

10.   Natural Law theory is a complex historical and philosophical topic and I do not pretend to illustrate this complexity in my paper. For helpful studies of this philosophical/theological position with many historical versions see: A.P. d'Entréves, *Natural Law*, London, Hutchinson Univ. Library, 1970 ed.; *Natural Law*, a theological investigation by Josef Fuchs, S.J., Dublin, Gill and Son, 1965; Jacques Maritain, *The Rights of Man and Natural Law*, London, Centenary Press, 1944; John Finnis, *Natural Law and Natural Rights*, Oxford, Clarendon Press, 1980. For analytic discussion of this theory in its history, philosophical problems and application to Ireland see: Desmond Clarke, *Church and State*, Cork, Cork University Press, 1984; especially chapter 2.

11.   St. Thomas Aquinas, 'Reason and Revelation' in Volume I, *On the Truth of the Catholic Faith* trans. by Anton C. Pegis, New York, Doubleday and Co., 1955.

12.   *Ibid.*, Aquinas is discussing reasons why most humans have difficulty discovering the truth. Among these reasons are indolence, weakness of intellect and passion. Cf. Pius XI, *Mit brennender Sorge*, AAS 29, 1937, 159; 'By his reason man is able to read this law written in his heart, at least insofar as he is not blinded by sin or passion.'

13.   Standard moral analyses would agree that no moral conclusions can be inferred directly from a set of factual claims about any specific process of nature. David Hume in his *Treatise on Human Nature* states what he argues is a fallacy in attempting to deduce an 'ought' (moral judment) claim from 'is' statements (factual claims). The main point in my discussion is to make explicit that any move (inference) from processes of nature to moral judgments requires the additional assumption of specifically *moral* premises. These premises are often camouflaged or suppressed in discussions of morality. Only by making these suppressed value assumptions *explicit* can there be a beginning to discussion of moral disagreements.

14.   A case in point is the Catholic Church's statement of 1975 on 'Sterilization in Catholic Hospitals'. The document states: 'The following is absolutely forbidden . . . the official approval of *direct* sterilization is something *of its nature* — that is, intrinsically — objectively evil . . . any cooperation in sterilization is contrary to the . . . defence of the moral order.' For full statement of this Church document see: Austin Flannery (ed.), *Vatican Council II*, the Post Conciliar Documents, Dublin, Dominican Publ. 1982, 454-5. The contentious theory resting in the background of 'Natural law' morality is the set of assumptions which demand that human beings take a subsidiary and resigned role vis-a-vis existing processes of nature. Arguments are necessary to show that alterations of certain physical processes are justifiable by reference to a more

important value. In the case of sterilization, the value to be defended could be 'responsibility in child-bearing'. For a discussion of the fallacy of question-begging which is a serious problem for the validity of the Church's arguments on such issues as contraception or sterilization, see: D. Dooley and D. Clarke, 'Definitions and Ethical Decisions', in *Journal of Medical Ethics*, 3, 1977, 186-188.

15.   It is helpful, however, to understand all Church claims to be the *sole, true teacher* in the light of the historical evolution of the Church. Two readable but well-researched books on Church claims to authority and problems associated with those claims are: Avery Dulles, *The Survival of Dogma*, New York, Crossroad, 1982, and by the same author, *Models of the Church*, Dublin, Gill and Macmillan Ltd., 1976. This latter book is a constructively critical assessment of the Catholic Church in all its aspects. Cf. Nicholas Lash, *Voices of Authority*, London, Sheed and Ward, 1976.

16.   The topic of authority merits much study especially when human lives are so often regulated by, or even tyrannized by, alleged authorities of all kinds. The following studies look at authority in its many facets: psychological, institutional and social. Richard T. de George, 'Authority and Morality' in *Authority* (ed.) Frederick Adelmann, The Hague, Martinus Nijhoff, 1975, pp. 31-49; Jack Dominian, *Authority,* London, Darton, Longman and Todd, 1976; Karl Rahner, 'Institution and Freedom', in *Social Studies*, Vol. 1, No. 2, March 1972, 117-123; J. Yarnold and H. Chadwick, *Truth and Authority* (Commentary on the Anglican/Roman Catholic Commission's Report on Authority, 1977).

17.   For a discussion of 'moral authority' see references cited above as well as R.S. Peters, *Ethics and Education,* London, Allen & Unwin Ltd., 1970, especially chapters 7-11 incl. The notion of a 'moral authority' undergoes a radical change when societies move from a 'traditional' society to a more 'urbanized or industrialized' society. This shift is relevant to Ireland during the last century and the following readings help clarify the basic alterations in experience that result: Harry Bohan, *Ireland Green*. Social planning and rural development, Dublin, Veritas Publ., 1979; Daniel Lerner, *The Passing of Traditional Society*, New York, Free Press, 1958; Peter Murphy, 'Moralities, Rule Choice, and the Universal Legislator', in *Social Research*, Vol. 50, No. 4, Winter 1983, pp. 757-801; for probing discussions on religion as it relates to social and cultural identity see: Roland Robertson, (ed.), *Sociology of Religion*, Middlesex, Penguin, 1969.

18.   Apart from the notable study, *Infallibity* by Hans Küng, there is a detailed look at Church teaching on this subject in *Infallibility*, by Peter Chirico, London, Sheed and Ward, 1977. For a fascinating study which traces the historical development of Vatican power and control and attempts an appraisal of ecclesial power as 'moral power' see: Jean-Guy Vaillancourt, *Papal Power*, Berkely, Calif., Univ. of Calif. Press, 1980.

19.   It is also the case that qualities that characterize authority may vary with societies but it is accepted as a defensible generalization that the *less* a leader's authority is firmly rooted in a traditional institution, the *more* it will depend on continuing success, on ability and initiative to communicate to others. Many

would want to argue that long-standing institutionalized authority has a built-in tendency to *exclude* the dynamic and thrusting innovator. A worthwhile and perhaps instructive comparison can be made between maintaining creative viability of Church institutions and viability of business corporations. In both situations, there is the on-going task of convincing the 'consumer' that the institution or corporation has a message or product that the consumer believes will contribute to their well-being. See: Thomas J. Peters and Robert H. Waterman, *In Search of Excellence*, New York, Harper & Row, 1982.

20. Liam O'Flaherty, *A Tourist's Guide to Ireland*, London, Mandroke Press, 1930, 36-37.

21. For clarification of the complex interconnection between law and morality see the following: Louis Blom-Cooper and Gavin Drewry (eds.), *Law and Morality*, London, Duckworth, 1976; H.L.A. Hart, *Law Liberty and Morality*, England, Oxford Univ. Press, 1963; Patrick Devlin, *The Enforcement of Morals*, London, Oxford Univ. Press, 1965; with specific reference to Ireland see, Desmond M. Clarke (ed.), *Morality and the Law*, Dublin and Cork, Mercier Press, 1982.

22. In a democracy it is often expected that majority views will be evident in legislation of the country. However, when majority views can be shown to infringe on or exclude expression of basic human rights of any 'minority', then problems arise in defending the imposition of majority views in legislation. Two brief but lucid discussions of this majority/minority issue can be found in the Irish journals: *Social Studies*, 'Power Imbalance, the Key Socio-Political Problem of our Time', Vol. 2, No. 4, Aug.-Sept. 1973, 331-336; 'A Time for Renewal and Organization' in *Social Studies*, Vol. 1, No. 2, March 1972, 117-123. Both of these articles are editorial statements of the journal.

23. A look at the educational programmes of seminaries in Ireland would reveal whether and to what extent communication skills and the psychology of communication are professionally taught. Communication skills need, however, to be combined with attitudes sympathetic to genuine dialogue if a Church is not to be seen as negatively 'authoritarian'. A discussion on this topic is 'Communication and the Training of Priests' by Jim McDonnell, *The Furrow*, Vol. 35, No. 3, June 1984, 367-374.

24. It has been said somewhat facetiously but not entirely so by a woman theologian, 'If men became pregnant, contraception would be a Sacrament!'

25. See: Letty Russell, *Human Liberation in a Feminist Perspective — A Theology*, Philadelphia, Westminster Press, 1974; Carol Christ and Judith Plaskow, (eds.), *Womanspirit Rising*, San Francisco, Harper & Row, 1979; Margaret MacCurtain and Donncha O'Corrain, (ed.), *Women in Irish Society*, Dublin, Arlen House, 1978; Rosita Sweetman, *On Our Backs*, London, Pan Books, 1979; Catherine Rose, *The Female Experience*, Dublin, Arlen House, 1975.

26. Quoted in *Female Experience, op. cit.*, p. 43 from the study *Patriarchal Attitudes* by Eva Figes.

27. Speaking consistently about impoverished lives in Ireland are Sr. Stanislaus Kennedy and Brendan Ryan among many. Sister Kennedy edited the following: *One Million Poor: the Challenge of Irish Inequality*, (Baldoyle, Dublin, Turoe Press, 1981). Sister Kennedy's work on pilot schemes to combat poverty is

available and one can only hope, not being ignored by policy-makers. Brendan Ryan recently published an article in *Doctrine and Life*, 'The Priest of the Future: a Powerless Servant', Vol. 35, No. 1, Jan. 1985. Ryan discusses the concept of power as it relates to perpetuation of injustice and inequality. He writes: 'The final and most painful transformation will come with the recognition that perhaps even Christ's message is better articulated out of the experience of the oppressed than the reflections of the priesthood.' p. 10.

28. See: William Duncan, *The Case for Divorce in the Irish Republic*, Dublin, Irish Council for Civil Liberties, 1979; William Binchy, *'No-Fault Divorce'*, in *Morality and the Law*, (ed.) Desmond M. Clarke, Dublin and Cork, Mercier Press, 1982, pp. 47-56; Ralph Brown, *Marriage Annulment in the Catholic Church*, England, Kevin Mayhew Ltd., 1977. Some fine discussion on this topic occurs in the following Irish journals: Micheal Mac Greil, 'The Christian Family and Social Change', *Social Studies*, Spring 1983, Vol. 7, No. 2, pp. 116-126; Gabriel Kiely, 'Changing Nature of Marriage', *Social Studies*, Vol. 7, No. 2, Spring 1983, 110-115; Dr. Peter Birch (Bishop of Ossary), 'The Irish Family in Modern Conditions', *Social Studies,* Oct.-Nov. 1973, Vol. 2, No. 5, 485-497.

29. For the official statement of the Church's position on the issue of religious upbringing of children in mixed-marriages see: The newly revised edition, *The Code of Canon Law*, London, Collins Liturgical Publ., 1983. Canon 1125 states the conditions which must be fulfilled if permission for a mixed marriage is to be granted. I am quoting only one part of the canon but in no way altering the meaning: 'The Catholic party is to declare that he or she is prepared to remove dangers of defecting from the faith, and is to make a sincere promise to do all in his or her power in order that all the children be baptised and brought up in the Catholic Church' (p. 199). In Canon 1126 it is left to the Episcopal Conference in respective countries to 'prescribe the manner in which these declarations and promises, *which are always required* are to be made . . . (p. 199)'. An excellent series of articles was published from an International Consultation on Mixed Marriage sponsored by the Irish School of Ecumenics in Dublin in 1974: Michael Hurley, (ed.), *Beyond Tolerance*, The challenge of Mixed Marriages, Geoffrey Chapman Publ., 1975.

30. Jack Dominian discusses some of the wide-reaching effects of suppressed inquiry in his book, *Authority*, cited above in note 16.

31. Cf. Michael Adams, *Censorship: The Irish Experience*, Dublin, 1968.

32. Sean O'Faolain, *The Irish*, England, Penguin books, 1969 ed., p. 143.

33. Sources cited above in the discussion of authority are relevant here. For a sustained defense of the thesis that Church paternalism is incompatible with moral maturity see: Desmond M. Clarke, *Church and State*, Cork, Cork University Press, 1984. A lucid statement on this issue is given by Dr. Paddy Leahy in his article paradoxically titled 'The Case Against Toleration' in *New Hibernia*, Vol. II, No. 2, Feb. 1985, p. 15.

34. The process of dialoging is not simply sustained talk but represents more of a carefully learned *discipline* of listening with an open mind, listening not only to words but to expressions and gestures that carry significant messages in any conversation. A recently published statement on dialogue comes from Letty Russell

in her study: *Human Liberation in a Feminist Perspective — A Theology*, cited above in note 25. See especially chapter 6, 'Communion in Dialogue', pp. 155-182.

35. The Irish Catholic church will almost certainly be called on to *modify* its structures of communication, pastoral services and administration of State education if it is to re-gain diminishing credibility. Peadar Kirby develops this thesis in his book, *Is Irish Catholicism Dying?* cited above. Avery Dulles, in many of his writings, also makes a cogent case for on-going modifying, vitalizing and updating of institutional Church life *if it is not to become permanently moribund.*

36. See: Dr. Andrew Rynne, *Abortion: The Irish Question*, Dublin, Ward River Press, 1982; Dolores Dooley-Clarke, 'Abortion and the Law in Ireland', in *Morality and the Law*, (ed.) Desmond M. Clarke, Dublin and Cork, Mercier Press, 1982, pp. 31-46.

37. William Duncan, in his book, *The Case for Divorce in the Irish Republic*, corroborates the claim that not enough research has been done into the incidence of marriage breakdown in this country. The need for further research is again emphasized by Kathleen O'Higgins in her study 'Marital Desertion in Ireland', 1974, E.S.R.I. Broadsheet No. 9.

38. See references suggested in note 28 above.

39. There are endless discussions in the Irish media about the limping economy and dire predictions of 'no jobs' for the children of tomorrow. The fear is often voiced that our Government will have failed to provide work for the expanding population. There seems to be consistent evasion or non-recognition of the issue of population restraint as a 'moral' mandate. To my knowledge, Paul Tansey, the economist, has grasped the nettle in his columns on the Irish economy but the challenge to pursue this aspect of the problem is mostly evaded. Why?

40. I am *not* saying that the Roman Catholic Church as an institution is incapable in theory of relating morality to lived experience. In fact, the challenge to do this was voiced repeatedly at Vatican II but moves to re-vitalize the Church have, unfortunately, not made a marked impact on the Irish Church. The full story as to *why* this is the case is a complex matter but one that still needs to be told.

41. For a thorough discussion of this assumption and its debilitating consequences see: John Dewey, *The Quest for Certainty*, New York, G.P. Putnam's Sons, 1929.

42. *The Quest for Certainty, ibid.* See also John Dewey's study of traditional religions and their impediment to human maturity and responsibility, *A Common Faith*, London, Yale Univ. Press, 1934.

43. *Quest for Certainty* and *A Common Faith, op. cit.*

44. A wide range of readable and scholarly books are being written on ethics as applied to business, environment, medicine, mass media, economics, education etc. There is no dearth of material, but training in ethics which expands the focus of concern and sharpens skills at reasoning — this kind of training is virtually non-existent in Irish education.

45. The new curriculum for secondary schools currently under discussion does not seem to provide for broad and non-religious studies of ethics. The national perception of morality as limited to a very small domain of life cannot easily change without planning at the level of education. Some may feel that the end

result of training in non-religious ethics would be empty, moral eclecticism. This need not be the case. Rather, the result could be 'understanding commitment' to positions that speak to reason and human aspirations.

46.   *Quest for Certainty, op. cit.*

47.   See Professor Joseph Lee's paper, 'Centralisation and Community' in this volume.

48.   Dr. Wayne W. Dyer, *Your Erroneous Zones*, New York, Avon Books, 1976, p. 82.

5 *Leonard Wrigley*

Ireland in Economic Space

Introduction

Ever since August 1971, when President Nixon formally suspended the convertability of dollars into gold, and thereby ended an era — The Golden Age of the West — of sustained economic progress under an umbrella of international monetary stability, all industrial economies, including Ireland, have faced three major problems: first, how to develop a process to balance the distribution of income between labour and capital; secondly, how to improve the response capability of commercial organisations to unpredictable changes in demand, technology, and supply; and thirdly, how to reduce public expectations that society can get something for nothing, that there is such a thing as a free lunch, that a people can at the same time and for ever enjoy low taxes and abundant welfare.

These problems confront the industrial world everywhere. A major error Ireland repeatedly makes is the assumption the problems she faces are unique to her. What is true is the problems bear more intensely on Ireland because she is newly industrialised than on her industrial neighbours. What is also true, and it is enormously important we face this phenomenon, is Ireland's responses are much less effective than countries comparable to her in population size and physical resources. Ireland is the only small industrial country to suffer very high unemployment. Ireland is the only industrial country to suffer an almost complete lack of domestic-owned international trading companies. And Ireland is the only country in the world at large, to suffer a public debt exceeding 130 per cent of Gross National Product while at the same time suffering very high taxation. What gives point to these facts is that Ireland's response-ineffectiveness is getting worse, as may be seen by the trend for unemployment, public debt, and taxation for the present business cycle, the last peak, 1979, the trough in 1982, and the present peak, 1985, as in Table 1. Clearly, there is something fundamentally wrong in Ireland's economic behaviour.

What could that be? From the view of newly industrialising countries, as of newly-founded businesses, the most important decision is from whom to learn. No other decision is of even remotely comparable importance. All new societies, as all old societies embarking upon a new path, become progressively stronger or weaker according as their external model is itself strong or weak in relevant aspects. It is crucial to learn only from relevant success. Here, I want to convince you of two things: first, that Ireland's practice of copying England's economic arrangements is the root cause of Ireland's progressive illness. England is too large, too oil rich, and too enormously unsuccessful in relevant aspects to serve as a useful model for Ireland. Secondly, if Ireland sets aside England as an economic model and starts to learn from what is common to four small European countries, each of which is comparable in physical resources to Ireland yet immensely successful in the things that matter, Austria, Denmark, Finland and Switzerland, then she will surmount her problems and in the result can face the future with confidence, not fear; and hope, not despair.

Ireland Copying England

Let us begin with Ireland's practice of copying England. Naturally, as Ireland was subjected to England for over seven centuries, much

TABLE 1

IRELAND, BUSINESS CYCLE, 1979-85
Unemployment, Public Debt and Taxation in Per cent

	1979 Peak	1982 Trough	1985 Peak (Est)
Unemployment as % of labour force	6·2	10·7	18·0
Public Debt as % of GNP	88	100	130
Taxation as % of GNP	27·5	32·0	36·5

SOURCE: Employment and Unemployment in Ireland, ESRI; Proposals for a Plan, 1984-87, National Planning Board.

that is Ireland today will have been absorbed from England. And much that is so absorbed may have made Ireland better than otherwise. However, what happened under political bondage is not the issue here. For the present paper, what is the issue is Ireland's practice since political independence in 1921 of copying England's economic arrangements.

For the world at large, England has been enormously successful as a political entity. Much that came from England is amongst mankind's greatest treasures. Certainly, England's political behaviour has been a model for many countries. However, when the focus is narrowed to economic behaviour, a different picture is presented. For nearly forty years England's economic performance has been dismal. This is so even with the vast North Sea oil wealth. In 1945, England was second only to the United States for economic well-being. By 1985, England was 17th or 18th amongst the 22 industrial economies. England has not been able to make progress in the modern world of changing technology and international competition. Comparative studies make the point clearly. England's economic behaviour and performance can be compared with those of USA, Japan, Germany and France in relation to investment, economic growth, and export growth, also to return on investment and to gains and losses in market share in the traded (manufacturing exports) area for period 1953 to 1976, as in Table 2. The focus is on economic fundamentals. Table 2 enables comparative answers to such questions as: is England's (UK's) relative economic decline due to low investment or low return on investment or both? If low investment, did England spend her heavy money on private consumption or public consumption or both? If low return on investment, was this because commercial chips were bet on the wrong (slow growth) area, or on the wrong aspects (e.g. basic research rather than product design), or both?

Take the years 1953 to 1976, when the rest of the world was 'catching up' with the USA in technology. Table 2 presents England (UK) as a high consumption/low investment/low growth economy. For each country growth was higher in the traded (export) area than in the combined traded and non-traded area (GNP). But it was in the traded area that England had the slowest growth. In manufacturing exports, England heavily lost market share, particularly to Japan and Germany. England was uncompetitive during these years. The

TABLE 2

COMPARATIVE PROGRESS OF LARGE AND MEDIUM-SIZE
ECONOMIES, 1953-1976
(*average of yearly figures)

	Percent of GNP Spent On:			%Growth in GNP* percent	Marginal product- ivity of investm.	Growth in export volume percent	% Share of world export manufactures	
	Private con- sump*	Public con- sump*	Invest- ment				1953	1976
USA	62·0	21·0	14·5	3·2	0·22	5·9	26·0	17·0
Japan	52·0	9·4	30·2	8·6	0·28	16·2	4·4	14·0
Germany	56·7	15·6	23·7	5·0	0·21	10·0	10·9	20·5
France	62·3	13·4	21·9	5·0	0·23	8·8	9·8	10·0
UK	64	17·5	17·3	2·7	0·16	4·5	22·0	9·4

SOURCES: D. Kern, NIER, 1980, No. 92; A.P. Thirlwall, Banco, 1979; Money, J. Ball, Macmillan, 1980.

reasons can be made clear. For the main factors in international competition, product design, quality, marketing and on-time delivery, the Management Forum, using expert opinion, positioned each of the 22 industrial economies. With England and Japan, the relative positions were as follows:

	Design	Quality	Marketing	Delivery
England	19	16	16	21
Japan	1	1	1	1

It takes no genius to see that England has done badly in the precise situations that make for success in the high growth traded area. That was the position up to 1976. As a recent *Sunday Times* editorial makes clear, nothing has essentially changed since:

. . . even after five years of Thatcher government, the economic decline of Britain continues apace. Despite the progress that has been made, we remain an inefficient, uncompetitive nation, afraid of new technology, uncomfortable with competition, short on business enterprise and management flair, long on appalling unions, and still obsessed with class divisions that are the joke of the world. Since the end of the Second World War, we have not gone nearly far enough to root out these obstacles to growth, enterprise and jobs. In the result, the pound which was worth $4 in 1945 is struggling to stay above $1 today.

From that view alone, and leaving aside the question of difference in scale, England should be the last country from whom Ireland, with her need for international competitiveness, ought to learn economic arrangements.

But difference in scale cannot, in practice, be left aside. A flea is not a small elephant, it is another species of animal. Difference in scale means difference in kind. In 1985, the population of Ireland was $3 \cdot 4$ million, while for England it was $56 \cdot 5$ million, more than 15 times larger. For Ireland to copy England in economic arrangements cannot be equated with reason. England is too large an economy to serve as a model from which Ireland could usefully learn.

Yet learn England's economic arrangements Ireland did. It was not that Ireland made a strategic decision to do so. There was no public discussion. Ireland learnt England's economic arrangements because geographically she is close to England, economically she was tied to England, politically she was subjected to England and she was and is in intellectual bondage to England. Continual bondage is the most significant. It connects with habits from the past but is more than that. As Professor J. Lee has stated many times, Ireland is highly centralised. In enormous measure, Irish political and economic power is located in Dublin. It is the combination of habit and centralisation which makes the bondage. Habits are the essence. Habits are very important in Ireland, more important here than in any other western country. Habits from the way things were done long ago, from the flow of authority — Westminster to Dublin Castle to the baronies of the Pale and beyond — remain as a living force to shape the minds of Irishmen in Ireland. Ireland never cut the bonds to England as Finland did to Russia. Through these bonds, England's economic arrangements enter Dublin and, because Ireland is highly centralised, are transmitted forceably to every corner of the land.

Economic Arrangements: Industrial Relations System

For economic effect on Ireland, the impact of England may be illustrated by reference to the industrial relations system. Competitiveness in such factors as product design, quality, marketing and delivery depend very much on good industrial relations — on people in business enterprises working well together — as is documented by research on the factors underlying Japan's export success. It is useful, therefore, to understand the main aspects of the English system, see how it came into Ireland and its impact on the Irish economy.

At the heart of the English industrial relations system are the trade unions. In England, trade unions developed during early industrialisation as a natural outcome of the class system — essentially, the 'haves' and 'have-nots' — and of England's intellectual preoccupation with the distribution of wealth, as distinct from its creation. English trade unions still bear the hallmark of their birth pangs. They always adopt an adversary role in negotiations. Trade unions are not just for high wages but also for job security. In the 1970s, when there was a shortage of particular skills in England, the trade unions used their power to give all workers a freehold to their jobs through the mechanism of the Unfair Dismissals Act. Consequently, workers cannot be fired except in extraordinary circumstances. Moreover, because workers cannot be fired, employers are reluctant to hire workers. Indeed, for a new business the hiring of a worker constitutes a major investment decision. Trade unions also create inflexibility in the labour market. Workers will not drop their wages to save their firm from an adverse change in the market, and unemployed workers cannot offer their services below the established wage rate; they cannot price themselves into jobs. Yet, all of this might be accommodated if trade unions promoted a strong collective work ethic and an effective system of continuous industrial training and skill upgrading, but they do not do this, at least they have not done this since the late 1960s. The inevitable result of England's trade union dominated industrial relations system is very high wages for those who are employed and, as the world becomes more competitive, very high unemployment.

This system was carried into Ireland along three different routes. First, Ireland replicated on a miniature scale the English trade union structure, a structure based upon 60 distinct craft unions. Secondly, Ireland inherited or reproduced English labour legislation, for example, the 1906 Trade Dispute Act, and the Unfair Dismissals Act of 1977. And, thirdly, Ireland adopted the class attitudes of English workers because for a long period England and Ireland constituted one labour market, with free movement of Irish workers to and from England.

An immediate and obvious result of copying the English industrial relations system was that Ireland suffered the full effect of the English wage explosion in the 1970s. This had a terrible effect. Yet, in those years Ireland was moving from an agricultural to an industrial economy and also was lowering the tariff walls to enter the world of international competition. Irish wages mechanically rose along with the English wages. No allowance was made for competitive difficulties facing Irish business following EEC entry in 1973 or the time required for new Irish business to become efficient. Irish wages rose far beyond what could be afforded without subsidies by Irish businesses in the areas exposed to full international competition. Irish firms in textiles, footwear, clothing and furniture, were made bankrupt; hundreds of Irish firms closed down, and tens of thousands of Irish workers became unemployed. Ireland lost her domestic-owned industrial base.

Another result was to make the hiring of labour a high risk investment. In field research on why employers would not take on more labour — the crucial question of today — businessmen responded along three negative dimensions. First, with job protection legislation, the employer bore a disproportionate share of the risk; the worker could leave at his pleasure but could not be compelled to leave; secondly, wage costs were always upwards, never downwards; and thirdly, if the market disappeared, redundancy payments had priority claim on the capital assets. Employers do continue to hire labour, but very carefully so.

Ireland as a Trading Nation

The full consequences of Ireland working on English wage rates are only now becoming clear. To provide high wage employment for workers from the bankrupt Irish firms or from the ranks of school-leavers, Ireland as a trading nation had to become a tax haven for American multinationals intent on the EEC market. The IDA was the vehicle. In choosing multinationals, the IDA identified computers and fine chemicals both as areas of international growth and as industries where links on the production chain from research through production to marketing could be geographically separated. Ireland was held out as a tax haven for assembly plants for computers or processing plants for fine chemicals. Early and even subsequent success has been enormous. No less than 80,000 jobs — at high wages — have been created this way.

But employment created in this way has significant costs. The American subsidiaries pay no taxes on their profits in Ireland. There is not, as in other countries, a huge tax base in the profits from the business sector. The tax load falls heavily on the PAYE workers. Moreover, these subsidiaries are truncated businesses, links along a chain, with no marketing or design functions in Ireland, so Ireland is not acquiring from its multinational subsidiaries the crucial skills for international competition, that is, skills in product design, quality, marketing, and on-time delivery. And, because of the transfer pricing practice of the multinationals, which price low their supplies into Ireland and high their outputs from Ireland to continental EEC markets, Irish exports, as measured by prices, are artificially bloated, causing a dreamworld effect in Ireland. More than all that, if ever there is a change in the tax laws in the United States relating to tax havens (more exactly to the time when tax has to be paid to the USA Revenue Authorities on profits made — or allegedly made — abroad) then Ireland's present industrial strategy would fall apart.

Of course, there are Irish-owned companies which trade abroad. The food cooperatives, for example, are important exporters, but the exports are of commodity nature, and depend on EEC price support and subsidies. At any time, these price supports and subsidies can be changed or eliminated depending on EEC politics. Food cooperatives cannot reasonably be seen as international trading companies. Indeed, they are in danger of becoming merely devices for exploiting the EEC.

From this view, the most massive fact about Irish industry is the absence of Irish companies that are truly competitive on the international marketplace. The rare exceptions, such as Biocon, Irish Distillers, Guinness, and Waterford Glass simply highlight this fact. Ireland today as a trading nation has become little more than a tax haven for American multinationals and an EEC subsidised commodity food producer. In both roles she is everyday gambling on external politics.

Ireland's Political Market
In theory a mixed economy combines the vigour of private enterprise and the virtue of collective action. But its weakness is that it contains two logically different markets, the economic market, where the businessman deals with budget constrained customers, and the political market, where the politician deals with voters who may believe their appetites for collective goods will be fed by other people — their lunch comes free. In a mixed economy when citizens are not

knowledgeable, collective action swamps private enterprise.

This swamping happened in Ireland. Twenty-five years ago, there were 1,020,000 people with jobs in Ireland; today the number is 1,060,000. There has been virtually no growth in the number of jobs. The economy has grown. From 1960 to 1985, annual average growth of real GNP was 4 per cent, which placed Ireland in the top half of the 22 industrial economies. This growth arose from increased labour productivity brought about by improved capital assets and by labour transfer from agriculture to public and private services. However the trade unions, under the umbrella of a vote-sensitive government, used their power to take productivity gains, not in lower prices, which would have increased job numbers, but in increased wages, which increased job rewards.

What also happened was the sense of business, vital for any trading nation, got lost. Over the twenty-five years to 1985, Ireland invested heavily in herself. The annual average investment was 25 per cent of GNP. Taking growth at 4 per cent, the average productivity of new capital assets was $0 \cdot 16$, which by reference to Table 2 is low by international standards. Much of the investment was in welfare infrastructure and much of the capital was invested by public authorities and financed by public borrowing. Since the return was low, public debts piled up. Ireland became a high consumption/high public investment/high growth/low profitability country. That is why she has not increased the number of jobs but has increased the public debt. In the institutional and behavioural structure of Ireland, the economic markets took second place to the political market.

Unemployment and Competitiveness

Economists insist that the laws of economic behaviour operate as vigorously in Ireland as they do elsewhere and, therefore, explanations of Ireland's economic problems ought in the first instance be structured in terms of the behaviour of the economic markets which make up the Irish economy — which include the markets for goods and services, for labour and real capital assets, and for money and financial assets — which requires a distinction between economic factors and the institutional and behavioural structure in which these economic factors are embedded.

This distinction has been drawn in recent studies of Ireland's economic problems. The most notable of the studies are the ESRI's

'Employment and Unemployment Policy for Ireland' and the National Planning Board's 'Proposals for a Plan 1984-87'. Both see Ireland's main problems as unemployment, government deficit, and competitiveness in the traded area, and relate these problems to downturn in demand due to world recession, increase in labour supply due to population fertility, and high factor costs due (in substance) to monopoly power over price. Both provided operational recommendations in respect of government deficits in terms of holding public expenditure stable. However, neither saw a solution within the foreseeable future to the problem of unemployment, in both areas their recommendations in respect of factor (including labour) costs must be deemed non-operational within the existing institutional and behavioural structures.

In highlighting the nature of these problems, the distinguished authors of the studies performed a service to the nation. But for the student of institutional structures three questions immediately present themselves:
1. Are there other nations comparable in population size and physical resources to Ireland which have faced and solved the same problems?
2. Along what dimensions did their solutions proceed, and can these solutions be learn by other nations? and
3. What is involved in the learning process?
Before looking at these, however, it seems necessary first to consider the notion of institutional — including nation state — learning.

The Notion of Institutional Learning

All higher animal species rely upon more than their genetic code for survival: to live, they must learn. Mankind is the obvious example, and human learning has been much studied down the ages, particularly since the social contract writers, notably John Locke and J.J. Rosseau. By contrast, the notion of institutional learning, that is deliberate copying of another institution's behaviour, has received much less attention. Of relevance here are two formal studies — the first by Wrigley (Harvard 1970) of corporate industrial learning, and the second by McKevitt (UCC 1977) of community spatial learning — and two well documented cases of natural learning, Germany and Japan in the period 1945 to 1970.

Wrigley studied the pattern of corporate growth and development in the United States. His model firm was opportunity driven and had a capacity to learn from relevant success. That capacity was the 'core skill . . . collective in character . . . the habits and knowledge of people who work together, who know and trust each other'. Firms were equipped with two radar systems, the first to pick up signals of market opportunities, the second to pick up signals of competitors who had succeeded in exploiting an opportunity. Most firms did not themselves work out how to exploit opportunities, rather they simply followed the relevant success of other firms. McKevitt studied the spread of the cooperative movement in north County Cork. His model community learnt from adjacent — not distant — success. Essential to McKevitt's model was 'community feeling' which may be taken as analogous to Wrigley's 'core skill'. Common to both models is the idea that institutional learning is in response to opportunities or problems, and effective learning requires both an information transmission system and a motivation and social capacity to absorb and exploit the information.

The best documented cases of national learning are from Japan and Germany, the once so-called miracle economies. Following the Second World War, these two defeated nations could see American technology was far higher than conceivable to them from the potentialities in their existing skills. So they make the strategic decision to catch up with America by learning American technology. (Monetary stability arising from the Bretton Woods agreement promoted this kind of long term vision). Each of these countries learnt just that set of technologies related to their existing skills. This was to ensure a future comparative advantage in the selected area. Technology was transferred by licensing, joint ventures, personal transfers and formal studies. These countries learnt not just in the sense of acquiring information, but of so organising themselves the information was transformed into changed economic behaviour resulting in new enterprises, new products, and new markets.

The implications of this successful learning have an importance that cannot be exaggerated. If a backward nation can learn from an advanced nation then progress is something that can be made. The significance of deliberate learning derives from the rise to dominance of the knowledge industries, such as electronics. These are now the main components of international trade. Historically, nations traded with each other in accord with their endowment of physical resources. Today, the basis of trade is human resources. Different countries developed their human resources to specialise on particular products: America for area engineering, computers, fine chemicals, and commodity foods; Germany for chemicals, and upmarket cars; Japan for popular cars, electronics and heavy engineering; Switzerland for watches and precision engineering. The comparative advantage of these countries arises from their set of institutions and behavioural practices which enable them acquire a special excellence in a selected industry. That advantage originally came from taking America as a model.

Models for Progress

In searching for a model for Ireland, the essential criterion is similarity in these areas that dominate progress. Here, for Ireland, three criteria are obvious. First, the model country, like Ireland, should be of that size where all the important people know each other and feel part of a 'family'. As a first approximation, this suggests those economies which have a population under ten million. Beyond that population size, no 'family' feeling is likely, for the various social strands will be too numerous and disparate to be brought together. Secondly, the model should correspond to Ireland in physical resources; that is, be neither richly endowed nor totally destitute. And, thirdly, the model country has to be further along the path to progress than Ireland, particularly in per capita income and employment and in surmounting the general problems of the industrial world.

On the first of the criteria, size, the world's twenty-four industrial nations can be culled to nine, namely, Austria, Denmark, Finland, Iceland, Luxembourg, New Zealand, Norway, Sweden, and Switzerland. Each of the nine are below ten million in population. Without question, in each of these countries, all the decision makers feel part of a 'family'. From Table 3 it will be noted that all these seven small economies have, relative to Ireland, lower unemployment, and, significantly higher per capita income. It will also be noted that Ireland apart, each improved its international competitiveness during the recession.

However, on the second of the criteria, the seven can be culled down to four countries, Austria, Denmark, Finland and Switzerland. All four, like Ireland, are deficient in natural resources,

TABLE 3
MAP OF IRELAND IN ECONOMIC SPACE
Unemployment, Population Size, and General Structure

22 OECD COUNTRIES*	Million Population 1982	International Competitiveness 22 = Lowest 1 = Highest		Labour Force Growth % 00	GDP per capita 1982 $US	Percapital real GDP Growth % average	Centralization: Public Administration** Ranking in 22 OECD Countries 1 = lowest 22 = highest	Collective Bargaining 1 = High 10 = Low	Unemployment as % of Labour Force			
		1982	1983	1976-81	1982	1977-1982			1982	1983	1984 Est.	1985 Est.
US	231·99	3	3	2·4	13047	0·59	5	9	9·5	9·6	7·5	7·3
Japan	118·38	1	1	1·2	8855	3·66	6	8	2·4	2·6	2·5	2·3
Germany, EEC	61·64	4	4	0·5	10652	1·71	3	5	6·1	8·2	8·0	7·8
France, EEC	54·22	15	15	0·7	9937	1·64	14	8	8·0	8·4	9·5	10·5
UK, EEC	56·03	13	14	0·3	8363	0·34	12	8	12·5	11·6	11·5	11·3
Italy, EEC	56·28	18	17	1·3	6178	2·15	21	8	8·9	9·7	10·0	10·3
Spain	37·94	17	19	-0·1	4758	0·33	13	8	15·9	17·9	19·5	20·0
Turkey	46·79	19	20	1·4	1122	0·27	-	-	14·5	15·4	16·3	17·0
Belgium, EEC	10·00	14	13	0·5	8446	0·98	17	5	13·0	14·0	14·5	15·0
Netherlands, EEC	14·31	5	10	1·7	9651	0·11	19	5	9·5	14·2	15·0	15·5
Portugal	10·09	22	22	1·4	2279	3·09	15	-	8·0	9·3	11·3	11·5
Greece, EEC	10·00	21	21	2·2	3817	1·49	18	-	5·8	6·1	6·8	7·5
Australia	15·2	7	12	1·6	10509	1·63	11	4	7·1	9·9	9·3	8·8
Canada	24·63	6	11	3·0	11750	0·48	2	9	10·9	11·9	11·3	11·0

TABLE 3 (Cont.)

22 OECD COUNTRIES*	Million Population 1982	International Competitiveness 22=Lowest 1=Highest		Labour Force Growth %00 1976-81	GDP per capita 1982 $US	Per capital real GDP Growth % average 1977-1982	Centralization: Public Adminis- tration** Ranking in 22 OECD Countries 1=lowest 22=highest	Collective Bargain- ing 1=High 10=Low	Unemployment as % of Labour Force			
		1982	1983						1982	1983	1984 Est.	1985 Est.
Austria	7·54	10	7	0·4	8846	2·01	9	2	3·5	4·3	4·5	5·0
Finland	4·83	8	6	0·9	10000	3·29	8	5	6·1	6·1	5·8	5·3
Norway	4·12	12	8	1·6	13689	2·56	10	3	2·6	3·3	3·3	3·3
Sweden	8·33	9	5	0·8	11837	1·28	4	3	3·1	3·5	3·0	3·0
Switzerland	6·45	2	2	0·8	14853	1·29	1	2/8	0·4	0·9	0·8	0·5
Denmark, EEC	5·12	11	9	1·4	10918	1·10	7	4	9·7	10·6	9·7	9·5
New Zealand	3·17	20	18	1·1	7666	0·90	16	5	5·3	5·5	6·5	7·3
Ireland, EEC	3·48	16	16	1·8	5057	1·97	20	8	10·7	14·1	16·8	18·0

SOURCES: OECD, Management Forum, Blyth and Clegg, Ministry of Finance, Denmark, Finland.

* Excludes Luxembourg EEC and Iceland.   **Per cent of tax revenue attributed to Central Government, 1981.

but not destitute. On the third of the criteria, all four have per capita income much greater than Ireland, between twice and three times as much; and their unemployment is much lower.

If we see what is common to all four, there are important things to be learnt. For there does exist a significant difference between what is common to all four and what does not strongly exist now in Ireland. Most obviously what is common is a tremendous sense of responsibility. The ideal of each is the responsible society, in the sense that all citizens feel responsible for their country and are made to feel very involved in decisions on progress. It would be remarkable, for example, for any of the four governments to produce plans without prior discussions. In these four countries, government plans are the outcome of discussion, they are the record of agreement for specific action. Also in these four, there is great concern to arrive at a consensus in matters of critical importance, particularly in industrial relations. Indeed, the word consensus itself is often used in these countries rather than a local translation. For each of the four, consensus is not a theory of culture but a daily practice accomplished by giving top priority to human relations. Problems are approached with consensus in mind. Given a national problem, there is an exhaustive preparation where all aspects are rigorously analysed by all those concerned before a decision is made. This means plan implementation runs according to schedule and fairly smoothly.

It is most noticeable that all four nations invest heavily in human resources to develop excellence in business and technological skills. Each of the four see their major resources as their work force, the technical skills of the workers, the specialist competence and organisational capacity of the managers, and the way these skills are related to the area selected for comparative advantage in the international market place. However, here two aspects should be noted: first, each of these countries specialise on products that are related in technology — they do not seek to be good at everything; secondly human resource development is the employer's responsibility — as a broad generalisation, about 3 per cent of corporate income is spent on education and training of the workforce.

The overall strategic concept of all five is internationalisation, that is they develop their products from the beginning to trade in the international market — they accept the need to live in the real world of commercial competition for market share. They focus on producer

TABLE 4

INTERNATIONAL COMPETITION:
RANKING AMONGST 22 INDUSTRIAL NATIONS

Country	Design	Quality	Marketing	Delivery
Austria	12	3	17	7
Denmark	5	4	6	4
Finland	10	10	11	8
Switzerland	4	2	5	2
Ireland	21	18	22	18

SOURCE: Management Forum Report, 1984.

goods, and here they are all good in at least two of the four critical success factors, as can be seen in Table 4. Of course, each of these countries do have notable consumer goods. But the industrial heart of each is in related producer goods.

Their notion of strategy is priority, more exactly the proper *sequencing of investments*, so they puzzle out the best order to do things. This necessarily limits the social agenda at any one time. All four have a few *strong trade unions* which are also involved in great matters of state.

Except for Switzerland, *changes in currency exchange rates* are not endowed with special meaning but simply a way of either reducing inflation as in Austria, which revalues its currency; or reducing export prices, as in Finland and Denmark, which devalue to remain price competitive in exports. The four are very skillful in economic and financial affairs. Keynesian ideas are applied in terms of counter-cyclical policies (for example, Finland used infrastructure development during a depression, balanced by tax on exports during booms). However, the ongoing economic emphasis is on improvement in business efficiency, that is, on the supply side of the econ-omy. The people in each of the four have a strong work ethic. Employers take pride in holding on to their workers, and are quick to have school leavers (though less so with long term unemployed). All four improved significantly their international competitiveness in the 1980s. Above all, all of these four nations operate as small, decentralised nations, that is all the top decision-makers, naturally, seek to get to know each other: they see their county as a nimble flea in a herd of elephants. By the same token, they go quietly about their business, and make good money and good jobs for themselves in the process.

Two other aspects should be noted in what is common to these four countries, decentralisation, and learning from relevant success. Decentralisation is a broad term, designed more to catch the flow of life than to define it. Perhaps in essence it means that local communities look after themselves and, in the best meaning of the phrase, mind their own business. With this in mind, measuring decentralisation along a number of dimensions gives the relative position of each of the countries as follows (where 1 means most decentralised, and 22 least decentralised of all 22 industrial economies in regard to public administration and to industry dependence on the Government):

	Austria	Denmark	Finland	Switzer-land	Ireland
Public Admin.	7	11	8	1	22
Industry	13	7	6	1	22
Average	10	9	7	1	22

Of course, these measures, if pressed, become simplistic and ultimately absurd. But if they are not the basis for minute scholarship, neither can they be dismissed entirely. They do represent a very large difference in the way Ireland is governed from the way that these four countries are governed.

The second aspect also to be noted is the immense vigour these four countries display in learning from relevant success. The Nordic countries — Denmark, Finland, Norway and Sweden — go to immense lengths to keep abreast of each other's success. So too do the various communities in the region centered on Switzerland, Middle Europa, which includes Switzerland itself, Austria, Bavaria and Northern Italy. In relation to Nordic Europea and Middle Europa, the only other region in the world comparably willing to learn relevant success is the Pacific Rim, including Japan, Taiwan, Korea, Hong Kong and Singapore.

In sum, the similarities of these four countries are consensus, investment in human resources, internationalisation of enterprise, an ongoing emphasis on supply side efficiency; a sense that 'small is what they are', decentralisation of decision making, and a willingness to learn from relevant success. If Ireland were to follow their path to success, these are the things she would have to learn.

NOTES

Theses:

F. Allen, The Irish Cheese Market, MBS Thesis, Published by the Management Department, UCC, 1985.

D. McKevitt, The Diffusion of Agricultural Co-Operatives in South-West Ireland, 1889-1931. Unpublished Thesis, UCC, 1977.

L. Wrigley, Divisional Autonomy and Diversification, Unpublished Doctoral Thesis, Harvard University, 1970.

Articles and Books:

R.J. Ball, *Money*, Macmillan, 1982.

P. Jay, 1976, 'A General Hypothesis of Employment, Inflation and Politics', Institute of Economic Affairs. Occasional Papers.

D. O'Mahony, Industrial Politics in Ireland, No. 19 C No. 24, E.S.R.I., 1963.

Lord Kaldor, 1971, 'Conflicts in National Economic Objectives', *The Economic Journal*.

OECD, Economic Surveys, all 22 Industrial Economies, 1960-84.

ESRI, 1984 Employment and Unemployment Policy for Ireland.

National Planning Board, 1984.

J.J. Rousseau, *Emile*.

J. Locke, *Civil Government*, 1964.

L. Wrigley, Foreign Direct Investment in Canada. Published in Corporate Power in Canada, Government Press, Ottawa, 1976.

L. Wrigley, 'Ireland: A Global Perspective', in *Towards a National Strategy*, An Foras Forbartha, Dublin 1983.

6 *Joseph Lee*

Centralisation and Community

Politics has been a vocation of the Irish since that great political entrepreneur, Daniel O'Connell, manager supreme of the passions of a people, pioneered the age of popular politics amongst us. But it was, naturally enough in the circumstances, the politics of opposition that we mainly mastered during the period of English rule. The Local Government Act of 1898 did confer some authority on local politicians, but they soon earned an unsavoury reputation for jobbery, even by the indulgent criteria of the folk culture, as they dutifully attended to the three F's of popular politics — family, friends, and favours. After 1921 the higher civil servants in the early Free State contemplated with mandarin disdain the corruption and incompetence that they associated with local government, and resolved to centralise administrative authority, as far as politically possible, in Dublin.

This attitude persisted even during the age of de Valera.[1] The Chief himself cherished an idyllic image of the self-reliant rural christian community, as he never tired of proclaiming.[2] But the process of centralisation continued inexorably under his aegis. He brushed aside the criticisms of bureaucratic centralisation by the Commission on Vocational Organisation, which sought structures of governance that would permit wider participation in decision-making.[3] There was a glaring gap between the platform cult of the self-reliant community, and the stern realities of the centralising state.[4]

The state did seem to finally vindicate itself in the economic surge of the '60s, a surge largely due to the injection of dynamism into a moribund administration by T.K. Whitaker and Seán Lemass. But this was a once for all development. It could not be repeated in that form. The economy and the society, which were hitherto relatively simple, became increasingly complex. As polities become more complex, administrations must become more flexible, or else bureaucracy will choke initiative. As the Irish civil service grew at unprecedented speed in the '60s and '70s,[5] it became less rather than more flexible. We now have an exceptionally centralised state by OECD standards, with central government accounting for not only an exceptionally high proportion of total national expenditure but also of total public expenditure.[6] Many individual civil servants have given dedicated service to the state. But administrative rigidity is now damaging decision-making, by politicians and administrators alike, paralysed by the institutional sclerosis that afflicts over-centralised organisations. The intervening years have only too sadly vindicated Tom Barrington's prediction of 1970 that 'The centralised system is likely to break down at a faster rate than it is even breaking down at present', resulting in a drift 'towards a bureaucratic neo-feudalism where the elected government would not be in effective control of the process of government'.[7]

The perspective of government has also been subtly distorted by the growth of Dublin. In 1926 Dublin city and county contained 17% of the population of the state. Today, they contain more than 30%.[8] That is exceptionally high by European standards, where the metropolitan area normally accounts for less than 20%, or roughly the Dublin proportion of 1926.[9] If Dublin related to Ireland as Paris — notoriously domineering Paris — relates to France, it would now have less than 700,000 people instead of more than one million. We have to go to Athens and Greece to find a Dublin-Ireland situation in Europe, and beyond that to the Third World.

Even the population factor does not fully reflect the growing dominance of Dublin over the mind of the country. A host of institutions, AFF, AFT, ESRI, IMI, IPA, IPC, IIRS, NBST, NESC, etc., have sprung up since the '50s. However worthy their work, their virtually axiomatic location in Dublin contributes to a centralisation of intellectual resources unique in northern Europe.[10] Except for a handful of isolated individuals, all our opinion makers now live in Dublin.

The coming of Telefís Éireann powerfully reinforced this growing pervasiveness of Dublin influence from the early '60s. There is a congenial self-image that RTE has helped to universalise Ireland, dragging the retarded indigenous inhabitants into the main stream of the twentieth century. But what RTE has really done is not so much to open the country to universal influences, as to act as a conduit for very specific, and in their own way often very provincial, Anglo-American ones. For we import little, at least via TV, of the best of the great English-speaking cultures. Indeed, the provincialism pervading so much of the nominally metropolitan milieu itself derives from this confusion of universal with mere Anglo-Saxon. Other European countries also import powerful external influences. But these countries nurture vibrant native cultures. They weave Anglo-American threads into the texture of their cultures, without, at least so far, rending the basic fabric. But our cultural personality is so fragile that the deluge of imports threatens to obliterate rather than invigorate our identity.

If the growth of Dublin were the result of fundamental economic forces, it might be argued that this simply reflected the dictates of economic efficiency. But the growth of Dublin since independence is due more to political forces than to economic ones. On a preliminary estimate, and despite the difficulties in the calculations, it would appear that the centralisation of administration in Dublin accounts, directly or indirectly, for a quarter of the capital's population, more than a third of its purchasing power, and the bulk of its opinion power. Only five of the more than eighty government departments and state agencies have their headquarters outside Dublin.[11] It is political will more than economic necessity that determines the location of a state city five times the size of Galway. And government continues to pursue a silent strategy of centralisation. All governments may say the opposite, but we must forget the platform platitudes about 'balanced national development'. The NESC has already referred to the palpable lack of measures to implement the alleged regional policy of 1972.[12] The service sector is now officially scheduled to account for the bulk of growth in future employment. But the service sector is disproportionately located in the Dublin area, partly because of the voracious state market at its door. The primacy of the service sector means, by definition, the continuing centralisation of power, wealth, influence and population unless there is a resolve to counteract this tendency by a far-reaching policy of decentralisation. And there is little sign of that. As an NESC report has summarised the situation, 'The absence of any effective or realistic ruban regional policy with regard to white collar jobs and information activities in this small, centralised and open econmy has left such activities no viable alternative to a Dublin location'.[13] In addition, even within the manufacturing sector, the shift in IDA strategy from job creation to wealth creation has potentially dangerous implications for regional development, given the difficulty of keeping wealth within the regions in which it is generated. The wealth created in the regions is peculiarly vulnerable to the suction effect of Dublin.[14]

To avoid being vulgarly misrepresented, however vain the hope, let me stress that I am not engaged in the puerile exercise of petty provincial denigration of Dublin. The country needs a capital of which it can be proud. Dublin is more symptom than cause of the problem. The problem is the centralised state. Dublin itself has fallen victim to that state. A bigger Dublin has not brought a better Dublin. More has meant worse. The crazy rush to pack another 200,000 people into the Dublin area in the past fifteen years has resulted in a decline in the quality of life for many citizens. The general quality of metropolitan life has coarsened, and outside the privileged precincts of the state class, the city suffers from a host of horrible problems.[15] As Michael Bannon, James Eustace and Mary O'Neill have rightly said, 'The scale of physical dereliction and human deprivation in Dublin . . . is a *national* scandal'.[16] Dublin itself must be saved from the consequences of excessive centralisation. Ireland may be a small county, but it is a long, long way from Ballsbridge to Ballyfermot.

Allowing for all this, are we still not too self-flagellatory? Has not the drive towards centralisation given us the twenty-sixth highest standard of living in the world? Should not mere Paddies feel gratified to bask in the glow of this improbable achievement? The historical record, unfortunately, gives occasion for pause. Fourteen northern European states are members of the OECD. Twelve of these cluster together in a first division in terms of income per head. Then comes one second division team, about a quarter behind the average income per capita for the twelve. That is Britain. And then comes one final team, fourteenth out of fourteen, all on its own.[17] There would be no third division in northern Europe if we hadn't created it. And it is our creation, not our inheritance. For we have fallen far back since independence. In 1921, Britain was out in front, and the rest of us clustered very closely together.[18] We were broadly abreast of the northern European field sixty years ago. Now we are lumbering along far behind. Had we achieved average northern European growth rates in the intervening period, we would now have double our standard of living.[19]

We are regularly reminded that we are burdened with the most rapidly growing population in Europe — or, more correctly, in the EEC. For more than a century we had the slowest growing population in Europe. That too was reputed to be a heavy burden.[20] We speak of population as if we are in no way responsible for our population patterns. They are apparently the unforeseeable consequences of the peculiar flight patterns of the stork![21] Readers will no doubt recollect the panic that seemed to spread among politicians during the 1970s when Brendan Walsh's work predicted population developments that not only followed as the logical consequences, but were indeed a central objective, of the economic policies of the '60s. Our capacity to be surprised at the predictable would be engaging if it were not so revealing of the calibre of the official mind. We are also now regularly warned that Europe is stagnating, and that it is the thriving economies of America or Japan we should strive to emulate. But the ministerial day trippers who understand little of America and less of Japan refrain from reminding us that their population is surging ahead at rates much closer to ours. But apparently they lack our talent for turning a growing population into a burden.

We cannot avoid the conclusion that we have incomparably the worst record since 1921 of any economy in northern Europe, except the British.[22] Our recent performance appears even more dismal if we concede validity to the 'catch up' hypothesis, according to which more backward economies have the possibility of growing more rapidly by learning the lessons, and benefitting from the achievement, of more successful ones.[23] We are now perched, through our own efforts, at the wrong end of virtually every relevant league table. The absolute gap between average northern European incomes and our own is as wide as the absolute gap between our own and African averages.[24] The first pre-requisite for improvement must be to recognise the dimensions of the problem, and to admit just how deeply disappointing has been our economic performance, not just in the recent splurge of collective inanity, but for far longer. Even the growth of the '60s, however impressive by our own previous performance, still fell below northern European averages. Having recognised reality, we must then proceed to search for explanations, not for excuses.

Several unusual features both symbolise and reinforce our third division performance. We take them so much for granted that they are part of what we are. We have the most sparsely populated inhabitable country in northern Europe, with only a fraction, as Table 1 records, of the population densities of other comparable northern European states.[25]

TABLE 1

	Inhabitants per square kilometre of land area
Netherlands	346
Belgium	323
Germany	248
United Kingdom	230
Switzerland	146
Denmark	119
France	98
Austria	89
Ireland	49

Sweden, Norway and Finland do record much lower densities than Ireland, but not when their uninhabitable areas are taken into acount. It is striking how little attention we pay to our unique position in this regard. We have apparently succeeded in persuading ourselves that our pre-Famine population of more than six million in the twenty-six counties was somehow an aberration, and that half that population somehow represents normalcy, when in fact it is even more of an aberration.

It seems doubly curious that a country in these circumstances should have chosen to pack so high a proportion of its exceptionally sparse population into one centre. While it must be readily acknowledged that influencing the location of population, and in particular countering the magnetic attraction of the metropolis, poses daunting problems for policy-makers, the relative success of measures adopted in Sweden and France, as well as the peculiar Austrian experience, suggests that the question revolves around political and bureaucratic will as much as technical economic factors.

In Sweden, concern came to be expressed about the 'excessive' rate of growth of the capital as the Stockholm area doubled its share of national population between 1900 and 1960, although the Stockholm region still accounted for less than twenty per cent of total population in 1960. Partly as a result of policy measures prompted by fear of growing concentration, the drift towards the Stockholm area has been halted. Göteborg and Malmö began to recover relative to Stockholm in the '60s, and by the end of the decade more people were migrating from Stockholm to Malmö than vice versa. The proportion of total population in the greater Stockholm area has stabilised in the past twenty five years.[26]

In France, Paris has long enjoyed a legendary dominance over the resentful provinces. Between 1856 and 1936, the Paris region accounted for eighty-seven per cent of total French population growth. The debate provoked by Gravier's famous book of 1947, reinforced by political pressure from the roused regions, stimulated policy initiatives that stabilised the size of greater Paris at less than twenty per cent of total French population. Chequered and reluctant though much French regional policy has been, nevertheless the trend of the previous century has been significantly changed since the Second World War.[27]

The Austrian case is unique. Vienna's role shrank from being capital of a multi-national empire before 1918 to being capital of a small state afterwards. In 1910 Vienna accounted for thirty-six per cent of the population of present day Austria. This has now declined, mostly since World War II, to twenty-two per cent.[28] The fall has been due more to actual population decline in the greater Vienna area than to rising national population. It can be safely assumed that a proposal to reduce the Dublin proportion of the Irish population from thirty per cent to twenty per cent would be denounced by many economists as a transgression of economic law, bringing economic doom on a society capable of perpetrating so unnatural a deed. Austria has not only survived a decline in Vienna's proportion of the national population. She has prospered.

In the northern European context, then, we appear exceptionally centralised, demographically distorted, economically backward, and, I would argue, culturally exceptionally derivative, and intellectually exceptionally dependent. No northern European country so misallocates its own intellectual resources, or relies so heavily on intellectual imports. Consider the case of the new theology, economics.

Thirty years ago, there were scarcely twenty professional economists in the country, nearly half of them outside Dublin. Now there are over three hundred, more than ninety per cent in Dublin. We have never had so many technically trained economists. But too many of them are technicians rather than thinkers. They tend to derive their assumptions from whatever the prevailing Anglo-American conventional wisdom may be. Unless they have good enough minds to stand back from their own training, they lack the capacity to assess their own assumptions. As a result, we who rely so heavily on imported ideas don't even know how to import ideas properly. We do not know how to learn. When we ask what makes other economies function, we so lack perspective that we frequently fail to choose the right economies to study. We often fail to realise that economies are so integral a part of societies that we must first ask what makes other societies function. We don't know how to ask that question abroad any more than at home. The result is that we incongruously combine geographical concentration of research institutions in Dublin with growing intellectual fragmentation between them. The individual institutions are responsible for understanding only individual parts of the social engine. It is nobody's responsibility, except residually that of the harassed politicians and civil servants, to understand how the pieces fit together, or what makes the entire system function. The rapid growth in consultancy work likewise tends to focus the minds of our economists even more obsessively on the short term — on providing instant prescriptions for immediately perceived symptoms. Again, technique inevitably tends to substitute for thought.[29]

Ireland suffers from an exceptionally low rate of return on her physical investment.[30] We have little idea of the rate of return on our intellectual investment. I suspect that a good deal of the gap between our long term growth rate and that of northern Europe can be explained by our inferior organisation of our intellectual resources. We ignore not only at our cultural peril, but at our material peril, basic research in the humanities and social sciences on the nature of our own society, placed in a disciplined comparative context. To confne ourselves solely to management studies, whose 'relevance' can be assumed, it seems reasonable to suppose that if a minuscule fraction of the millions pumped into subsidies for industry had been made available to minds as probing as Professor Leonard Wrigley's to think about economic strategy, it would have repaid itself handsomely as a national investment. Our university system is so organised that much of the time of our best minds is squandered on minutiae. Professor Wrigley himself, for instance, who is internationally recognised as one of the seminal minds in management studies since his famous Harvard doctorate, calculates that only ten per cent of his time is available for creative thinking.

The juvenile, if euphonic, phrase, 'paralysis by analysis', has been coined to dismiss the apparent plethora of published reports perplexing policy-makers and commentators condemned to the agony of reading. By northern European standards, it is the paucity of publication in the policy sciences that distinguishes us. We have the paralysis all right. But it is not from a surfeit of analysis. Most of the reports are not analyses at all. They are merely technical exercises in tunnel thinking, devoid of serious reflections on their own underlying assumptions. It remains true that 'much discussion tends to be about solutions to problems that have been inadequately defined'.[31] The most striking lacuna of all in our intellectual activity concerns analysis of the state itself. The nature of the Irish state has become quite central to the nature of our society. In no northern European country does the state play so pervasive a role. And in no northern European country has so little analysis been devoted to the role of the state. It is a distinctive phenomenon in its own right that we neglect serious enquiry into understanding the linkages between the several distinctive features of our social organisations.

A Cork resident has to be conscious of how the local community has been decimated by factory closures in the early '80s. It has arguably been even more seriously decimated over the years by the exodus of talent to the centre. 'Black spots' like Cork must then endure the condescension of futile central task forces — as if the representatives, however individually able, of an arthritic system can instantly produce magic formulae to invigorate Cork — or Castlebar, or Waterford, or Wexford, or wherever is to be blighted next. Instead, these centres must suffer the further psychological damage of having decisions made ostentatiously for them, rather than by them. The recruitment of talent from the provinces to the capital is up to a point a normal and desirable development, and all the more so if it be part of a circular flow. Even in its one-way state, it might be justified in the national interest, if only it delivered the goods. It hasn't.

Is there an alternative orientation? Or are we doomed by some inscrutable decree to a position of eternal inferiority? The proposition that the Irish are inherently inferior, for whatever reason, in matters economic, or even in general behaviour, must be calmly considered. Some apparently feel that Sir John Junor, the *Sunday Express's* gift to political thought, somewhat over-reacted to recent vibrations in Anglo-Irish relations by championing so enthusiastically the honour of his porcine friends. But is it really possible to defend the Irish against charges of slovenliness, selfishness, and general incapacity to think in terms of the public good when we look, for instance, at the litter dump we have made of our little country — and imagine what a garbage heap it would be if we had European population densities! We must indeed wonder if it will not be left to a later generation to break the link between Paddy and the pig.[32] But litter is only a symptom of our wider domestic malaise. It is the performance of our people abroad that most effectively refutes the inherent inferiority argument. As a people, we do have our fair share of talent. It must then ultimately be our organisation of that talent at home that condemns us to falling so far below our potential. Why do we so lack the talent to use our talent?

The lack of a sense of community, sacrificed on the altar of state centralisation, helps foster among us the familar 'rights without responsibilities' mentality. The state has connived — with our willing, not to say eager, collusion — at turning us all into suppliants on its centralised largesse, providing sinister but seductive support for the debilitating effect on national character of the 'something for nothing' syndrome. The challenge now is how to mobilise the individual abilities, and the individual generosity of the Irish people, reflected in their response to the Colin McStay appeal, or to the Ethiopian famine fund, for collective public purposes.

Most successful countries operate relatively decentralised decision-making systems. Irish emigrants have flourished in the decentralised states of the USA, Canada and Australia. The most successful big state in northern Europe, West Germany, and the most successful small state, Switzerland, in both of which the central government has normally been responsible for less — often for much less — than fifty per cent of the total public expenditure,[33] leave far more initiative and control over resources to subnational authorities than we do. So do several other successful small states, including Denmark, Norway, Sweden, Finland and Austria, in all of which regional and local authorities account for a much higher proportion of total public expenditure than with us.[34]

And their systems are not the result of immutable natural laws. The view is frequently found in Ireland, for instance, that the German Länder are 'historic' entities, stretching back to the teutonic forests, and that they occupy their place in the German governmental structure in response to clamant public demand. That is simply not the case. Only three of the nine Länder can claim historic legitimacy. And public opinion in the early Bundesrepublik wanted a centralised state.[35] It is not, then, as if European societies are inherently superior. These societies face their own problems, and they are far from depriving their public men of the pleasure of caressing the body politic. But they still work consciously at creating effective decision-making structures. They think.

But decentralisation isn't good enough for Ireland! It is scoffed at by the wise men as cumbersome and inefficient. Why? Partly, of course, as a rationalisation of the natural lust for power and desire for personal comfort.[36] But intellectually and emotionally it is because we have conditioned ourselves to think English. Indeed, in many respects we have bettered the imperial instruction. The irony is that England herself has declined from a position of economic primacy and fallen into a second division. We have imported 'the English disease' without having taken the precaution of achieving the preceding English state of health, which might postpone the debilitating impact of the disease. It took the English at least three centuries to mould Ireland in their own centralising image. If we want to remake it in a distinctive Irish image, we have to work at it. It will take time. We must begin by resisting the instinct to imitate England, not necessarily because it is England — that would be as vulgar a mark of the serf mentality as the customary mindless imitation — but because so much of it is now, sadly, second rate. To finally escape from the English shadow, we must fashion a new sense of political, cultural and economic space for ourselves.

Many place their faith in 'technology' as the key to the future. And we must indeed become more alert to the potential of technological change. But our main problems aren't mainly technological. Even the choice of priorities among which technologies to domesticate, while it cannot be made without sophisticated technological advice, is not primarily a technological decision. Our problems are as essentially intellectual, cultural, administrative and political as they are technological. They have to do with the way we organise our abilities and our institutions, and indeed our technologies. For it is arguable that we are far from having devised the most effective means of harnessing the potential of technologies and technologists for our future social development.

The IDA has followed a fairly active policy of industrial decentralisation. But it has to run hard to stay in the same place until the location of public decision-making is also extensively decentralised. Until we recognise that a fundamental cause of our failure lies in excessive centralisation, then all other efforts to create a viable national society will falter. Not all the IDAs, all the EECs, all the multinationals, can change that basic truth. There may be occasional recoveries, even spurts or 'bonanzas'. They will make no fundamental difference.

In the short term, we continue to need foreign investment. The misadventures of some multinationals should not divert attention from the fact that we have many very fine foreign firms here. But it is so much easier to import investment, to warp the educational system to provide concealed subsidies for birds of commercial passage, than it is to endure the upheaval of fundamental institutional reform. We need a shift in our whole mental axis, but not one that sacrifices our residual scraps of identity for nothing better than servility to subsidised squatters, instead of fostering the self-reliance that requires an education of intellect, imagination and character. When the foundations are fragile, the frantic effort devoted to keeping up the paint work is doomed to futility, however lucrative it may be for the decorators of the day.

The first steps towards a solution to our longer term difficulties lie in the re-organisation of the state, and in raising the standards of citizenship by forging a sense of community. A healthy sense of community can act as a catalyst, but community can be claustrophobic as well as liberating. It can be as elusive in reality as it is alluring in imagery. It will have to be understood, and worked at, if it is to succeed. It is usual to argue for community on grounds of equity, and for centralisation on grounds of efficiency. There is a strong argument from equity, not least from christian concepts of equity, for the fostering of community values. Indeed, the failure of the Catholic Church in Ireland, the repository of some of the best intelligence in the country, to provide a sufficiently robust body of social doctrine to challenge the power of bureaucratic centralisation, remains one of the great lost opportunities of Irish intellectual endeavour.[37] But in this essay I am deliberately not arguing from a romantic vision of Ireland as a hazy haven of bucolic bliss in a frenzied modern world. I am arguing on the chosen ground of the centralisers. By their own criterion of efficiency, they have failed. Indeed, the more one contemplates the comparative trajectories of European performance, the more meretricious does the claim of centralised efficiency appear. The stage has now been reached where the internal colonialism of the centralised state has to be smashed before the true potential of our people can be unleashed.

To cure the long term paralysis, we need a creative synthesis between state and community. That is why I, for one, refuse to join in the fashionable chorus of condemnation of Knock airport. Knock is apparently to cost about £12 million. The waves of centralised indignation we have had about Knock contrast with the deafening silence about 'a new runway . . . for Dublin airport at an estimated cost of £30 million'.[38] The runway may well be desirable, but it has wended its discreet way into the national plan ('a final decision on the investment will be taken later by the government') without as much as the raising of a solitary plucked eyebrow. More revealing still has been the silent condoning of the waste involved, from a national point of view, in crowding 200,000 more people into the Dublin area in the past fifteen years. And then, as the quality of life deteriorates, we require Criminal Justice Bills to deal with the victims of a system that never gave many of them a chance. I am not competent to assess the technical arguments about Knock. But if Knock is wrong, the £12 million is a drop in the ocean of centralised waste. And if Knock is even half right, it has a chance of vitalising a community. Right or wrong, if this country is to flourish as a distinctive identity, it will owe far more to the faith and energy of the Msgr. Horans than to the myopic perspectives of their detractors.

There is no infallible system of government, adapted to all political cultures at all times. Whatever the merits of centralisation at an earlier period, central government can no longer claim the clear superiority in either competence or integrity over possible alternative systems (not necessarily the existing system of local government) that may have justified its earlier accumulation of powers. The distance between the state and the citizen is now provoking a dangerous degree of apathy, if not of alienation, and frustrating the possibility of participation in decision-making.

Decentralisation cannot ensure vibrant community development. It is not a panacea. Much depends on the type of decentralisation. But it is an essential prerequisite for the sustained improvement of national performance into the twenty-first century. Because central government dismisses so disdainfully the case for decentralisation, little serious thought is devoted to devising an effective system of decentralisation. The present local authorities are far from ideal. But then, how can they be expected to display initiative or behave responsibly when they are deprived of any incentive to do so? The missing link between centralisation and community is civic culture, or what Mr. de Valera called 'the standard of citizenship'.[39] It seems doubtful if that can be raised until the citizen acquires more authority over his own affairs.

Our young people have not come out of the womb stamped third class, as those of us who enjoy the privilege of teaching some of them well know. Despite the relatively meagre resources which the universities enjoy by northern European or north Atlantic criteria, many of our students are still able to compete with the more fortunate graduates of much better endowed systems. But they deserve something better than the increasingly fashionable injunction to emigrate. There are circumstances where an emigration policy can contribute to the good of both the society and the individual. Where an economy would seem to have reached its maximum potential, and to be suffering from 'objective' over-population in relation to any reasonable expectation concerning its prospects, then an emigration policy can be justified. But, unless my argument about Irish potential be hopelessly wrong, and we are much closer to our ceiling than I believe, that is not the case with Ireland today. In our situation, those who advocate emigration, however well meaning their motives, are essentially seeking a mandate for mediocrity. There is no reason, except the refusal to tackle head-on our own inadequacies, why emigration should be necessary from so sparsely populated a country. The standard of citizenship cannot be raised until citizens have something to feel part of, and feel proud of, until they can share a sense of place and a sense of collective identity. A state that seems to embrace the soft option of emigration cannot hope to inspire self-restraint in its citizens. Restraint for what? To sustain the convenience of decision-makers who resist the reform of a discredited system?

The Irish public are often reprimanded for harbouring excessive expectations. But how can our expectations be excessive when we lag so far behind northern European averages, and when so much remains to be done to provide decent educational and cultural opportunity, not to mention economic opportunity, for our people? Far from being too high, our expectations for ourselves are far too low. Unfortunately, partly because of our fixation with second rate English standards, partly because the suffocating role of the centralised state saps initiative,[40] our expectations of ourselves are also sadly low.

The younger generation will live to see the centenary of our independence. Will they have nothing better to look back on than the blighting of the high hopes and generous impulses of youth? Are they to be yet one more Irish generation that shrivels slowly into the corrosive cynicism of the disillusioned, as the sap dries in the bough and the leaf withers on the branch? Is it all to have been for nothing better than that?

It ill-behoves the historian, above all others, to succumb to the mood of the moment. Despite the prevalent disillusion, there are still high stakes to be played for in our country's history, north and south. And that history, though it be but the history of a small country, though it be marred by too frequent policy failures, though it be demeaned at times by sordid acts and squalid episodes, still remains the history of a people who, despite copious and insidious instruction, have yet to learn to consciously bow the knee. However small and open an economy we may be, our fate, barring major war, still lies largely in our own hands. It would be a historic achievement if the coming generation, by breaking the grip of the bureaucratic state, began to salvage the squandered talents of our people, and redeem the bartered pride of our country.[41]

NOTES

1. For a classic expression, see Department of Local Government and Public Health, 'County administration', 1 March 1934, S.P.O. S 6466.

2. For elegant expositions of de Valera's thinking in this regard, see J.P. O'Carroll, 'Eamon de Valera, charisma and political development', in J.P. O'Carroll and John A. Murphy (eds.), *De Valera and his times*, Cork, 1983, pp. 17-34, and Gearóid Ó Crualaoich, 'The primacy of form: a "folk ideology" in de Valera's politics', *ibid.,* pp. 47-61.

3. Joseph Lee, 'Aspects of corporatist thought in Ireland: the Commission on Vocational Organisation, 1939-43', in A. Cosgrove and D. McCartney (eds.), *Studies in Irish history presented to R. Dudley Edwards*, Dublin, 1979, pp. 324-46; J.H. Whyte, *Church and state in modern Ireland, 1923-1970*, Dublin, 1981, pp. 96-119.

4. T.J. Barrington, *From big government to local government*, Dublin, n.d., p. 198.

5. Peter C. Humphreys, *Public service employment*, Dublin, 1983, pp. 53 ff.; T.J. Barrington, 'Whatever happened to Irish government?', in F. Litton (ed.), *Unequal achievement*, Dublin, 1983, pp. 97-9.

6. *Revenue Statistics of OECD Member Countries, 1965-1982*, Paris, t 88, p. 164.

7. T.J. Barrington, *From big government to local government,* Dublin, n.d., pp. 91-2.

8. W.E. Vaughan and A.J. Fitzpatrick (eds.), *Irish historical statistics 1821-1971,* p. 17; J. Blackwell, 'Some aspects of population change', in An Foras Forbartha, *Technology and the infrastructure: Ireland in the year 2000*, Dublin, 1981, pp., 11-18; NESC, 45, *Urbanisation and regional development in Ireland*, Dublin, 1979, p. 40.

9. The European percentages are deduced from data in Hugh D. Clout (ed.), *Regional Development in Western Europe*, 2nd ed., Chichester, 1981.

10. AFT does conduct research in provincial locations.

11. Brian Callanan, 'The work of Shannon Free Airport Development Company', *Administration*, 32, 3, 1984, p. 347.

12. NESC, 45, *Urbanisation and regional development in Ireland*, p. 51.

13. NESC, *ibid.,* pp. 259-60; N. Whelan, 'National and regional development', *Administration*, 28, 4, 1980, pp. 396-7, n 24, p. 407.

14. See the salutary warnings on this score in T.A. Boylan and M.P. Cuddy, 'Regional industrial policy: performance and challenge', *Administration*, 32, 3, 1984, pp. 255-70.

15. For perceptions of the present plight of Dublin, see *Sunday Independent*, 24 February 1985, p. 6.

16. NESC, 55, *Urbanisation: problems of growth and decay in Dublin*, Dublin, 1981, summarised in M.J. Bannon, 'Urban deprivation in Ireland with special reference to Dublin', in Council for Social Welfare, *Conference on Poverty 1981*, Dublin, 1982, pp. 288-311.

17. *OECD Economic surveys: Basic statistics: International comparisons.* Ireland's ranking within the EEC is almost as dismal. See Commission on Taxation, *First Report,* Dublin, 1980, t 7, p. 76.

18.   A. Milward and S.B. Saul, *The development of the economies of continental Europe, 1850-1914*, London, 1977, p. 515; L.M. Cullen and T.C. Smout, 'Economic growth in Scotland and Ireland', in L.M. Cullen and T.C. Smout (eds.), *Comparative aspects of Scottish and Irish economic and social history 1600-1900*, Edinburgh, n.d., pp. 13-14, and n. 16, p. 18; D. Aldcroft, *The European economy 1914-1978*, pp. 44-5.

19..   On twentieth century growth rates, see United Nations, *Economic survey of Europe in 1961: some factors in economic growth in Europe during the 1950s*, Geneva, 1964, ch. II, t 2, p. 3; Aldcroft, *op. cit.*, t 5.1, p. 163.

20.   See, for example, *Economic development*, Pr. 4803, Dublin, 1958, p. 11.

21.   The relationship between economic growth and population change is a highly complex one, and I do not wish to over-simplify it here. W. Black, 'The national plan: a northern perspective', *Irish Banking Review*, December, 1984, pp. 6-8, contains sobering reflections on the issue. In a broader context, however, what is striking is how little sustained attention most of our economists or demographers have devoted to the linkages.

22.   United Nations, *op. cit.*; S. Pollard, *The wasting of the British economy*, London, 1982, pp. 2ff.

23.   M. Olson, 'The political economy of comparative growth rates', in D.C. Mueller (ed.), *The political economy of growth*, London, 1983, p. 42; M. Abramovitz, 'Notes on international differences in productivity growth rates', *ibid.*, pp. 79-89.

24.   This is a moderate formulation of the implications of the OECD international comparisons.

25.   OECD, *Economic surveys: international comparisons.*

26.   Ella Ödmann and Gun-Britt Dahlberg, *Urbanisation in Sweden*, Stockholm, 1970, pp. 43-4, 54; The Swedish Institute, *The Swedish economy: facts and figures 1984,* p. 5; R. O'Connor, E. O'Malley and A. Foley, *Aspects of the Swedish economy and their relevance to Ireland*, E.S.R.I., Broadsheet no. 16, December 1978, p. 38.

27.   J.F. Gravier, *Paris et le Désert Français,* 1972. R.E.M. Irving, 'Regionalism in France', in James Cornford (ed.), *The failure of the state*, London, 1975, pp. 18ff. A survey twenty-five years later by Gravier, *Paris et le Désert Français en 1972*, Paris, 1972, struck a more hopeful, though still admonitory, note. Other useful examples of the lively French debate include, in addition to the titles listed by Irving, Jean Coppolani, *Le Réseau Urbain de la France: sa Structure et son Aménagement*, Paris, 1959; and Robert Lafont, *La Révolution Régionaliste*, Paris, 1967.

28.   F.C. Engelmann and M.A. Schwartz 'Perceptions of Austrian Federalism', *Publius* 11, 1 (Winter, 1981) n. 16, p. 87. See also B.R. Mitchell (ed.), *European Historical Statistics*, London, 1975, pp. 19, 78.

29.   For a welcome exception to this tendency, see Joe Durkan, 'The national plan', *Irish Banking Review*, December, 1982, pp. 18-19.

30.   OECD Economic surveys 1983-1984; *Ireland*, December, 1983, pp. 21-2.

31.   Barrington, *From big government to local government,*, p. 207.

32.   Bord Failte and the IDA now report that the litter situation is deterring tourists and industrialists from coming to Ireland.

33. G.C. Schweitzer, *Politics and government in the Federal Republic of Germany*, Berg, 1984, p. 177. W.E. Oates (ed.), *The political economy of fiscal federalism*, Lexington, 1977, p. 311.

34. *Revenue statistics of OECD member countries, 1965-1982*, t 88, p. 164. International comparisons of this type are notoriously tricky, but the orders of magnitude involved do seem to put these countries in a different category from Ireland.

35. *Informationen zur politische Bildung*, 204, 1984, pp. 11, 13.

36. If one seeks a less vulgar formulation, public choice theory will supply an appropriate vocabulary. See David O'Mahony, 'How should the plan be interpreted?', *Irish Banking Review*, December, 1984, pp. 30 ff. The negative responses of private sector office personnel to the idea of decentralisation is not so much to moving the work outside Dublin, as moving the workers. It is a way of life, not economic efficiency, that determines the response (NESC, 28, 1976, pp. 101-2). That is understandable. But it has nothing to do with national interest, public good, efficient performance, etc.

37. Lee, *op. cit.*, pp. 341 ff.

38. *Building on reality 1985-1987*, Dublin, 1984, 7.76, p. 147.

39. For further comments on this topic see my *Reflections on Ireland in the EEC*, Dublin, 1984, pp. 47-8, and 'Society and culture', in Frank Litton (ed.), *Unequal achievement: the Irish experience 1957-1982*, Dublin, 1982, pp. 1-18.

40. M. Ross, 'Comprehensiveness in Regional Policy', in B.R. Dowling and J. Durkin (eds), *Irish Economic Policy*, Dublin, 1978, pp. 297-333; D. Hannan and J.P. O'Carroll, *The sociology of regionalisation*, Cork, 1976; Bruce M. Logan, 'From vanguard to base camp: new perspectives in Irish public administration', *Administration*, 32, 3, 1984, pp. 271-93.

41. Many of the themes touched on in this paper are stimulatingly explored in the writings of Desmond Fennell, most recently in *The state of the nation: Ireland since the '60s*, Swords, 1983. I have also read with profit an unpublished paper by Frank Litton, which he has kindly placed at my disposal, 'A note on a comparative study of sub-national systems of government'. I am grateful to Ms. Mara Kuhne-O'Leary, a specialist on Japanese history in the Department of Modern History, UCC, for discussing the Japanese governmental system at length with me. To Ms. Charlotte Wiseman, Secretary in History, UCC, my debt on this occasion, as on so many others, is incalculable.

Notes on Contributors

William J. Smyth was brought up in the rural farming world of Bourney, near Roscrea in County Tipperary. He was educated at the Christian Brothers school at Templemore and at University College, Dublin. A Travelling Student of the National University of Ireland, he completed his Ph.D. dissertation while at the University College of Wales at Swansea. He lectured in the United States of America (Syracuse Univ., N.Y. and San Fernando State Univ., L.A.) and Canada (Winnipeg and St. John's, Newfoundland) before returning to University College, Dublin in 1971. He was senior lecturer and head of the department of geography at Maynooth College from 1973 to 1977, Dean of the Faculty of Arts there from 1975/77 and President of the Geographical Society of Ireland from 1975 to 1978. He has been Professor and head of the department of geography at University College, Cork since 1977. His publications are mainly concerned with the historical, social and cultural geography of Ireland as seen within the broader European and wider Atlantic (including Colonial American) framework. Apart from journal contributions, he has essays published in chapter form in *Ireland and France, Ireland: the Geographical Dynamic* and *Tipperary Essays*. He is also interested in and has published on the nature and philosophy of geography as a discipline. Chairman of the National Committee for Geography 1980-1984, he has been editor of the journal *Irish Geography* since 1981.

Seán Ó Tuama is Professor of Modern Irish literature in University College, Cork, and has been a visiting Professor in the universities of Harvard, Oxford, and Toronto. His publications include two books of his own verse and four plays, as well as literary criticism and literary history. *An Grá in Amhráin na nDaoine* (1960), *Caoineadh*

Airt Uí Laoghaire (1961), *Filí faoi Sceimhle* (1979) are amongst his most notable academic works, while *An Duanaire, Poems of the Dispossessed* (1981) — a bilingual anthology done in conjunction with Thomas Kinsella — attracted widespread attention. A prolific playwright, all of his nine plays in Irish have had public performances on stage, radio or television. He served as a member of the Arts Council from 1975 to 1981 and was Chairman of the working party which produced a report entitled *The Arts in Irish Education* (1979). In 1982 he was appointed Chairman of *Bord na Gaeilge*, and was deeply involved in the drafting of the *Bord's* four-year action plan for Irish, *Plean Gníomhaíochta don Ghaeilge* (1983-1986). At present he is engaged on a new book of literary essays.

Bryan M.E. McMahon was born in Listowel in 1941. He graduated from University College, Dublin in 1963 with B.C.L. and LL.B. Degrees (First Class Honours). He became a solicitor in 1964 and went on to obtain a Fellowship from Harvard Law School. He practiced law in Wall Street, New York, before taking up a teaching position in England in 1966. He began lecturing in law in University College, Cork in 1967. In 1977 he became Professor of Law and Head of the Department. He was seconded to the Law Reform Commission as Research Counsellor in 1977 and has been a Stagiare Professor with the Council of Europe on two occasions. He has just returned from sabbatical research in Oxford.

He is a member of several Committees including the Attorney General's Committee on Law Reform in Ireland. He has examined extensively for universities, professional bodies, etc. He has appeared twice as Legal Consultant before the Court of Justice of the E.E.C. (Luxembourg).

He has published and lectured extensively in the areas of Economic Law, Irish Law of Torts and E.E.C. Law.

Dolores Dooley lectures in the philosophy Department at University College, Cork. She did her undergraduate work in English, Theology and Spanish at Mundelein College in Chicago, Illinois; her M.A. at St. Louis University with a thesis on the 'Philosophy of Language in Ernst Cassirer'. She took her Ph.D. in Philosophy at the University of Notre Dame in South Bend, Indiana. Her dissertation was on the subject of 'Moral Dispositions' in the work of the 18th century German philosopher, Immanuel Kant. Dr. Dooley, who takes a special interest in educational philosophy and methods, administered a Carnegie-funded educational experiment in the teaching of philosophy in American secondary schools during 1967-69. She also taught philosophy at several U.S. Colleges before moving to Ireland in 1974. In 1978 Dr. Dooley was a visiting lecturer at Wolfson College in Cambridge where she continued her research in medical ethics. She has published articles in the areas of medical ethics and educational philosophy in the *Journal of Medical Ethics, Hastings Center Report, Journal of Critical Analysis* and *Philosophical Studies*. She holds membership in the Institute for Society, Ethics and Life Sciences, the American Philosophical Association, the Irish Philosophical Association, the Society for Applied Philosophy and the British Society for the History of Philosophy.

Leonard Wrigley is Allied Irish Banks Professor of Management and Dean of the Faculty of Commerce, University College, Cork. He was born in Glanworth, Co. Cork and was educated in Glanworth National School, London School of Economics (B.Sc. Econ.) and the Harvard Graduate School of Business Administration for a Doctorate in Business Administration. During the Second World War, he was an officer in the British Army from 1944 to 1947, served in France and Germany with the Parachute Regiment and was awarded the Military Cross in June 1944 and the bar to the Military Cross in March 1945. His industrial career includes Production Manager of Maconochie Foods. In the early 1960s, he was Industrial Adviser to the Government of Ethiopia and Chief Industrial Adviser to the Government of Iraq. He has taught at Harvard and Chicago, and was Chairman of the Business Policy Department in the School of Business Administration, University of Western Ontario. His main research and publications in North America have been in Corporate Strategy, and National Industrial Strategy, and in Ireland, on industrial strategies for chemicals, construction and foods.

Joseph Lee was born in Tralee in 1942. After graduating from University College, Dublin in History and Economics, he served as an Administrative Officer in the Department of Finance before being appointed Assistant Lecturer in History in UCD in 1963. He was awarded the Curtis Memorial Prize of the Royal Irish Academy and the Travelling Studentship of the National University before going to the Institute of European History, Mainz, to pursue work in German History. He took up a Research Fellowship in Peterhouse, Cambridge in 1968, and subsequently held office as Official Fellow, Tutor, College Lecturer, Tutorial Bursar and Director of Studies in Social and Political Sciences. In 1974 he was appointed Professor of Modern History in UCC, where he has also been Dean of the Faculty of Arts (1976-9) and Vice-President of the College (1982-5). Professor Lee, who serves on a number of national committees, has been Visiting Mellon Professor of History at the University of Pittsburgh, and Visiting Professor at the European University Institute, Florence. Among his publications on Irish and German history are: *The Modernisation of Irish Society 1848-1918* (Dublin, 1973), and 'Labour in German Industrialisation', *Cambridge Economic History of Europe, VII* (Cambridge 1979).

Further Reading

Readers who wish to pursue detailed references relating to the individual lectures in this book are referred to the end notes following each chapter. The short selection of titles listed below may be of use to readers seeking a more general view of issues recurring throughout the series.

Tom Barrington, *From big government to local government*, Dublin, n.d.

T.A. Boylan and M.P. Cuddy, 'Regional industrial policy: performance and challenge', *Administration*. 32, 3, 1984, 255-70.

K. Boyle and D. Greer, *The legal systems north and south (a study prepared for New Ireland Forum)*, Dublin, 1984.

Hugh D. Clout (ed.), *Regional development in Western Europe*, 2nd ed., Chichester, 1981.

P.J. Corish, *The Catholic community in the seventeenth and eighteenth centuries*, Dublin, 1981.

E. Estyn Evans, *The personality of Ireland*, 2nd ed., Belfast, 1981.

D. Fennell, *The state of the nation: Ireland since the '60s*, Dublin, 1983.

R. Flower, *The Irish tradition*, Oxford, 1947.

B. Friel, *Translations*, London, 1981.

S. Heaney, 'The sense of place', in *Preoccupations: selected prose 1968-1978*, London, 1980.

Irish Geography Jubilee Volume, Dublin, 1984.

B. McMahon, 'Developments in the Irish legal system since 1945', in J.J. Lee (ed.), *Ireland 1945-70*, Dublin, 1979, 83-95.

J.S. Mill, *On Liberty* (1859), London, 1974.

J. Montague, *The dead kingdom*, Mountrath-Port Laoise, 1984.

G. Murphy, *Ossianic Lore and romantic tales in medieval Ireland*, Dublin, 1971.

NESC, 45, *Urbanisation and regional development in Ireland*, Dublin, 1979.

NESC, 77, *The criminal justice system: policy and performance*, Dublin, 1984.

K. Nicholls, *Gaelic and Gaelicised Ireland in the Middle Ages*, Dublin, 1972.

B. Ó Cuív (ed.), *Seven centuries of Irish learning*, Dublin, 1961.

R.S. Peters, *Ethics and education*, London, 1970.

W.L. Rowe and W. Wainwright (eds.), *Philosophy of religion*, New York, 1973.

D.P.J. Walsh, *The use and abuse of emergency legislation in Northern Ireland*, The Cobden Trust, 1983.

L. Wrigley, 'Ireland: a global perspective', in An Foras Forbartha, *Towards a national strategy*, Dublin, 1983, 15-20.